Journey Into the Dungeons of Science

Also by Ashish Dalela:

Semantic Atomism
Semantic Reasoning
The Journey of Perfection
Material and Spiritual Natures
Conceiving the Inconceivable
The Science of God
Time and Consciousness
Conceiving the Inconceivable
The Balanced Organization
The Yellow Pill
Cosmic Theogony
Emotion
Mystic Universe
Moral Materialism
Signs of Life
Uncommon Wisdom
Gödel's Mistake
Quantum Meaning
Sāṅkhya and Science
Is the Apple Really Red?
Six Causes

Journey Into the Dungeons of Science

SHABDAVERSE
VOLUME 4

Ashish Dalela

Journey Into the Dungeons of Science —SHABDAVERSE Volume 4
by Ashish Dalela

Published by Shabda Press
press.shabda.co
ISBN 978-93-85384-52-3

SHABDA
PRESS

Contents

Series Preface

SHABDAVERSE is a series of article collections, organized by topics. The articles in these collections were originally published online on the SHABDA website over many years. A series of articles written from 2014 to 2019 were earlier published in chronological order under the series title *Western Questions Eastern Answers*. The SHABDAVERSE series organizes articles from 2019 to 2025 by categories, rather than dates. This is for multiple reasons—(a) there are enough articles in each category to produce collections organized by categories, (b) readers wanting to read topic-focused collections might find this approach more convenient and cohesive than the chronological one, and (c) the topic-focused approach allows us to make unique covers for each book, after all, in the ultimate analysis, a book is judged by its cover!

All these articles follow an interdisciplinary approach to every topic—everyday experience, empirical evidence, problems with different ideas advanced in the past and present, how ideas may have evolved historically, how certain issues were seen and understood differently across cultures, and with a solution to any and all related open and unsolved problems, which can be validated through ordinary experience, empirical evidence, and rational arguments. I often cite statements and ideas from Vedic texts, not to substantiate my claims, but to establish that my ideas are not new, and that I as the author of these articles don't claim authorship of the ideas. I only aim to present ancient ideas in a modern language, so that present audiences may understand and appreciate them based on what they already trust.

Pursuant to the science-religion divide created during European Enlightenment, we see two opposite approaches to the study of ancient texts—(a) the religious approach takes an ancient text as a divine revelation to be trusted on faith at best, and (b) the scientific approach, which rejects these texts as the personal opinion of dogmatic scribes, unprovable through or contradictory to the available evidence, and focuses on collecting evidence, followed by speculation to find an explanation that fits that evidence.

The Vedic tradition differs from both of these. Ancient texts have been preserved in a written form for thousands of years, but in every successive era, those texts were explained through commentaries. The texts and the commentaries were never merged. That trend continues today, and those who like to read ancient texts with explanations can do so. However, these explanations do not contrast their ideas with those in present-day sciences and religions, because the Vedic tradition was historically inward-looking, not outward-looking. By continuing the same trend, commentaries on Vedic texts appear to most people as different ideas, not better or true ideas, when contrasted to the ideas found in other worldviews. In fact, those ingrained in other worldviews consider Vedic texts primitive because the Vedic ideas don't match the ideas they have received through their culture and education. Therefore, the inward-looking historical trend of the Vedic texts is not adequate for the present time. For the present time, the Vedic tradition must become outward-looking, and contrast itself to the ideas of the other worldviews.

Therefore, in these articles, we—(a) sometimes we begin with unsolved problems created by prevalent ideas and theories and try to solve them using reasoning and evidence, and then connect the solution to the ideas in ancient texts, and (b) sometimes we begin with ideas and theories in ancient texts and show how they are relevant to the present time by showing how they solve unsolved or open problems.

I have seen with consternation a tendency among many authors to take ancient ideas, reformulate them in convenient ways, disconnect them from the sources from where these ideas were taken, and present these ideas as an author's original work. I think that this approach constitutes a theft, disrespectful to the teachers and texts from where ideas were taken. But more importantly, it filters the tradition of texts and teachers through the opinionated lens of the author who takes ideas without attribution, and closes the door for readers to go back to the tradition for more exploration in the future. Authors with such attitudes present themselves as prophets of original ideas, while masking the actual prophets.

I aim to show people of the present time a path to the Vedic tradition, not pretend to be a prophet of original ideas. Personally, I'm convinced that everything I have written about is a miniscule fraction of all that can be written, understood, or derived from the Vedic texts, and hopefully, future generations will do more of what I have tried to do. My primary goal is to dispel the myth that the Vedic texts are like the texts of other religions which have to be accepted on faith, rather than reason and observation. I call the dispelling of this myth, the *scientific study of Vedic texts*, pursuant to the common definition of science as truth based on reasoning and evidence, in contrast to a religion based on blind faith or belief.

Ashish Dalela

Artificial Intelligence and the Death of the Free Market

In classical economic theories, the "market" is an abstract entity, used by everyone, but owned by no one. It could be regulated by a government by enacting the rules and regulations of market transactions, but even the government did not own the market (unless it was the sole producer and consumer). In fact, nobody could say what the market really was, because every individual was part of the market.

But things have now changed. The markets are not free anymore. They are owned by the likes of Amazon, Google, Facebook, and other technology platforms. All these companies will tell you about the power of the free market that led to their rise. They won't say that they are now the market, that everyone else is a player in their control and they use that power to profit from all market transactions.

An Illustrative Example

Take Facebook for example. As you scroll down your Facebook feed, the software tracks the rate of scrolling. If you pause on something for a second, Facebook knows that you are interested. If you scroll faster, then Facebook knows that you are not interested. When you scroll randomly, then Facebook knows that you are anxious. When you dwell on negative posts, Facebook knows you are depressed. If you focus on positive posts, then Facebook knows you are in a happy mood. It uses all these behaviors to create your personal profile.

If you are depressed, you might not tell your family, employer, or friends about it, because you feel shy or embarrassed. But you will do things on your computer or phone by which Facebook can know your mental state, personality, likes and dislikes, thought patterns, and so forth. You think you deserve privacy, and you maintain your privacy by not telling your friends, family, and employers about your thoughts and feelings. You don't know (or don't care) that Facebook knows more about you than anyone else, simply because your finger movements create a personal diary available only to Facebook. So, they can read your personal diary, and use it to determine your nature and state.

As Facebook figures out that you are depressed, they will show you more depressing pictures. If it figures out that you are happy, then it will show you happy pictures. Many of the things that you see in your feed are *promoted content*. Which means someone is paying in advertising to make you see it. Classical advertising used newspapers, TV ads, radio ads, and so on. The prospective buyers of a product were 1% of all those people who read newspapers, watched TV, or listened to the radio. Software platforms like Facebook change that. Now, by tracking your personality, desires, and mental state, then can target prospective customers with products more effectively. By targeting, the advertiser has to spend comparatively less on advertising, as they are getting more "bang for the buck"—more views for less money.

Of course, it is not always easy to decode your mental state and personality from your finger movements. Therefore, Artificial Intelligence is touted as the technology which will create a system to determine your mental state and personality from the observation of your finger movements. By improving AI, Facebook will get a better grasp of your personality, moods, and thoughts, and target you better.

The Foundation of Artificial Intelligence

The specific technology underlying modern AI is called "Neural Networks". It is a network of nodes created in software that is divided into many layers. The logical nodes in each layer connect to the logical nodes in the next layer, and the connection is assigned a numerical weight—i.e., something between 0 and 1. When you give some input to a neural network, it triggers some nodes in the first layer, which then triggers the next layer nodes based on the connection weight. These triggered nodes then trigger multiple nodes in the subsequent layer, and this process continues for many layers until the final layer has been triggered. The greater the number of layers and nodes in a neural network, the more sophisticated it gets, which gives the neural network its power. The triggered nodes in the final layer are called the "output", and quite like the input, they are also a sequence of bits. Thus, the input is a sequence of bits, and the output is also a sequence of bits. The difference between Neural Network AI and the classical models of AI, which rested on programming logic, is very subtle.

In classical AI, people were trying to represent the knowledge of the world, and then program a logical procedure (called a program) to use that knowledge. The problem was that each domain of knowledge required a unique knowledge representation and program. For example, a surgeon needed a different system of knowledge and programs than an engineer. This made AI very *expensive* because it required expert surgeons and engineers to devote their time to producing a useful knowledge representation and programming the logic of their actions before AI could be effective. The Neural Network approach solves that problem. Now, you produce a single hardware and software system, and you give it to the experts—e.g., doctors and engineers—and they can "train" that system, which is a euphemism for setting node weights.

In this training, the doctors or engineers don't need to tell you about their mental models of the world, how they think about problems, or how they go about solving those problems. They can do all of that in their heads, and just tell the neural network about the solution for a given problem. When enough problems and solutions are provided, the neural network develops its own understanding of the doctor or engineer, which may be quite different than the doctor's or engineer's own mental models, but they produce the same results. Thus, the AI system is not identical to the doctor or the engineer, but it can *act* just like the doctor or engineer. The term "artificial" in AI is used to indicate this difference; the doctor's or engineer's intelligence is "real" while the neural network has "artificial" intelligence.

A neural network model for checking the grammar of sentences in the English language is a set of weights—between 0 and 1. English language neural network models are freely available on the internet and you can download such a model from the internet, install it as an input to your neural network software, and create an AI system capable of processing the English language. Effectively, you can have commodity computers, and commodity neural network software, and the only thing that matters now is the neural network model.

In this new age of AI computing, computer hardware, and software, are slowly becoming irrelevant. What is relevant is "data"—which is a euphemism for a neural network model—produced from a lot of training data, either given by experts or surreptitiously collected by observing human activities. When a model is created by experts, it is very expensive. But when it is created from the observation of human activities, then it is very cheap (for the collector). This cheap form of AI is dominant today, while expert-driven data models (such as to be used in self-driven cars) are still under development. However, the gaps between these two types of AI systems keep narrowing.

In the self-driven car neural model development, for example, a car is driven by the neural model, unless it makes a mistake and a driver takes control. If the driver does so, then it indicates that the software was doing something wrong. That is training for the software—to learn from the driver's actions—and reduce the time that the driver has to take control. If that metric is constantly on the decline, then the AI model is improving. This process can take years if not decades because the rate of improvement can get slower with time.

How Artificial Intelligence Is Deployed

Facebook for example can have many neural network models—one for each user, another one for people in a city, another one for people in a country, another one for doctors, another one for perverts looking to harass women, another one for drug dealers, another one for people undergoing medical treatment, and so on. The underlying hardware and software are the same—they implement a neural network. This greatly reduces the cost for the company doing the Artificial Intelligence because it can deploy the same hardware and software many times. The difference is simply in the observed data that is fed to "train" these models—sometimes continuously to evolve the model.

For example, the base model in Facebook is of each user. As you scroll your screen, you create a time series of hand movements, which is then used to create the neural network model of that user. Facebook constantly experiments with new users by showing them a wide variety of things. If you scroll past that post, then the neural network is trained to not show you such posts. If you dwell on it, click on it, like it, share it, or comment on it, then the model is trained to show you more such things. Once the model is trained sufficiently, then it can produce an output for any given input. The input can be a certain news article, and the output would be a number that indicates whether you will like it, share it, comment on it, or ignore it. So, a news article is now fed into user-specific models to decide if it will produce "engagement".

This per-user neural network model can also be used to create "meta-attributes" such as a doctor, engineer, drug dealer, sick, male, female, heterosexual, homosexual, etc. by comparing your responses to other neural networks previously trained for the above-noted attributes. For example, Facebook can get doctors into a room, give them a series of posts, and check their reactions. Through those reactions, they can train the "doctor" model. If your behavior is similar to the behavior predicted by the doctor model, then you are classified as a doctor. Each of these is a weight between 0 and 1, which means that in the perfect scenario, a doctor gets the weight 1 against the attribute "doctor".

In AI language, this is called "classification", which means that the AI system is putting you into many classes or categories. Once per-user behaviors and their meta-attributes (that classify these behaviors into categories) are determined, then these models are continuously improved through more data. For example, if you were initially classified as a doctor, but your behavior is slightly different from the standard doctor model, then the software will take your behavior into account as that pertaining to doctors, and modify the doctor model.

Thereby, there will be models of all doctors, all engineers, all perverts, or all drug dealers. Then, there can be intersectional behavioral models in which doctors in each country have different personalities, or drug dealers in different cities behave differently. There is literally no limit to how many attributes are incorporated in modeling and how many intersectional models can be created by their combination.

Again, you can input a certain news article into that model, and determine whether all doctors or all engineers will like, share, comment, or ignore that article. Based on that likelihood, Facebook can decide whether it should show that group of users that particular news article. Facebook can decide how effective this exposure to articles has to be. For instance, the advertiser who pays a lot of money to Facebook for publicizing a certain news article can get better treatment—i.e., they get more relevant and interested users who will like their article. Conversely, the advertiser who pays a little money to Facebook can be given worse treatment. Thereby, simply by the power of money, some content can be made "viral", and that popularity attracts even more people to it due to social validation. Facebook can also incentivize new customers by giving them much higher benefits initially and then tapering off their benefits slowly—so that they will have to pay Facebook more money in order to get the same benefits. It all depends on which behavior Facebook thinks makes the most money for them.

This money-making process is also a neural network model, which can be different for countries, cities, engineers, doctors, salesmen, and so on. And there can be intersectional models too. Thus the same amount of money produces different effects for different users.

Effectively, once you make your neural network software, all you need is a lot of computer hardware to instantiate that software many times and designate each such hardware-software combination as a machine that is training a different neural network. These machines then automate all business decisions to maximize the machine owner's profits. The personal, national, community, religious, and professional classification or modeling, help Facebook to target users selectively. And advertisers pay for that selective targeting of users, which helps Facebook make money, improve its software and models, and constantly manipulate both advertisers and users to increase its own profits.

Why Governments Can Do Little

As we have noted above, the neural network is just a set of numbers. If you give this network an input—e.g., a news article—the output is also a set of numbers. You cannot do anything with numbers alone; you have to be able to give these numbers an *interpretation*.

For example, if a neural network produces three numbers—0.9, 0.8, and 0.75—you cannot make anything out of the digits themselves. To know what these numbers mean, you must know that these three numbers correspond to an attribute tuple such as {doctor, American, rich}. This *interpretation* of numbers is embedded in software, proprietary to the company that creates the neural network model. Thus, the tuple of the three numbers above means that there is a "rich American doctor". Without that interpretation, numbers mean nothing.

Now, we have to know that software is "private property", which means that unless some national interest is involved, governments cannot look at a company's software. At best, they can say: This data was produced in our country, by the citizens of this country, so we have rights over it. But that doesn't affect Facebook, because Facebook can give the government terabytes of numbers—which is the "data" produced by the citizen's behavior and constitutes their behavioral models—and the government cannot figure out what those numbers mean. Effectively, the government cannot use that data the way that Facebook can, because the data is useless without the software interpretation.

So, all laws about data privacy are effectively useless. The government must have laws to compel Facebook to "cooperate" with the government which means giving them the interpretation of data rather than the data itself. Facebook will happily comply because they now know that the government depends on Facebook. The government asking for Facebook data is leverage for Facebook over the government. If the government doesn't give Facebook concessions, Facebook can turn off the data tap, say that they don't know, or give misleading information. The government cannot know whether Facebook is telling the truth or not. The governments know this very well; they cannot fight daily battles. If they antagonize Facebook, then they can get some data or interpretation, but it could be useless or misleading.

The Usurping of the Free Market

Effectively, the users who provide the data by their finger and thumb movements, are helpless. Their behavior is being modeled like guinea pigs under an experiment—feed this and you get this behavior, feed that and you get another behavior—and use that feeding to create a model of the guinea pig. The businesses who produce advertisements are helpless because they don't know to whom Facebook feeds their advertisements, and their profiles—i.e., whether Facebook is truly giving the bang for their buck. They just have to trust that Facebook is doing a good job, without the ability to verify what they are doing. Finally, the governments are helpless, because they have created privacy laws over software ownership, that give Facebook the power to do what it wants and keep the government on the tenterhooks.

I've used Facebook as an example. This is not unique to Facebook. It also applies to other large platforms like Amazon, Apple, Google, Microsoft, etc. They all track clicks, the text you type, and the fingers you move. They may also selectively share the data they have with others—for a price of course—and they just have to hide what they are doing in obscure legalese called the "terms of use", which nobody reads, but even if they read it, they can do nothing about it, except quit the platform. If many users move to a platform, then by quitting you only isolate yourself. Effectively, you are locked into the platform, and manipulated by the platform, to help someone else profit.

The classical free-market system was about producers and consumers, regulated by governments. Economics professors stated that the market was so complex that no single entity could control it. The market had to be kept free because that was the most *efficient* system of market operation. The inability of any single entity to control the market was the primary reason for the collapse of communism.

But now the erstwhile thesis that the market is too complex to control is disproven. The market can be controlled—by algorithms, software, and machines—by monitoring everyone constantly. Thereby, there is a fourth player—large software internet platforms—more powerful than producers, consumers, and the government in the classical free-market system. It is no longer a free market, because the software platform is the market within which everyone plays, and it is owned by a private business. One business owns the market, and users, businesses, and governments are tenants in the market. At best, their freedom comprises voting by their feet and quitting the tenancy, to their detriment.

The Cluelessness of Current Debates

There are many clueless people who still think that we are operating in a free market system. They talk about the excesses of large technology platforms and regulations to control them or consider this the choice of the free market that should not be tampered with. They either don't know economics or technology, or both. Their ignorance is overshadowed only by their hubris about technological progress.

Yanis Varoufakis calls this "techno-feudalism", reminding us of the times in Europe when the feudal lords owned the land, and workers tilled that land for the feudal lords. In India, this was called the Zamindari system, in which the Zamindar (the landowner) had power over the workers who tilled the land. But this analogy is deficient; the reality is much worse, because there used to be hundreds of feudal lords, and the government still had power over them (although the government may not have exercised that power). For instance, the worker could move from one feudal lord to another, and the government could take the land away from the feudal lord. Both these powers are now gone. You cannot quit Facebook, Amazon, Google, Microsoft, Apple, etc. to go to another platform, because the alternatives either don't exist or by changing the platform you lose most of your friends. Nobody can compete against their existing power. And the government is helpless.

So, you might think that the correct term is "techno-communism", where the technology platform is the communist government that controls everything—the people, businesses, and the bureaucracy. But even that term would be deficient because the communist rulers still had some form of socialism. The principle for large software platforms is simply increasing the profits for themselves and their shareholders.

You might like to say that the technology platforms are autocratic, with no constitution and rule of law except the profit motive, the goal to advance personal power, and then use it to increase profits even more. But even that analogy would be deficient because even autocrats had some responsibility to maintain law and order within the state. They had to ensure that the economy would not decline so drastically that it could lead to a revolution. The software platforms don't have that responsibility. They are just responsible for increasing their profits.

Thus, no comparison with the past is truly accurate or applicable to the current dilemmas. It is not capitalism, feudalism, communism, or autocracy, but the worst aspects of all of them. It has emerged in the heart of the technology industry, which prides itself as the beacon of progress and prosperity, operating under the principles of the free market, and democracy, as opposed to closed societies, or hereditary wealth.

This is important because people, businesses, and governments remain clueless about how to handle the problematic situation. They often look to the past and try to compare the situation to capitalism, feudalism, communism, or autocracy, but that is not enough. The government can use its powers to break down the tech behemoths, but that won't solve any problem because the separated entities will develop cooperative agreements, then cite increasing dependency on each other, and then merge back again. Any laws created to stop cooperative agreements, partnerships, or mergers will affect everyone else adversely. So, things that the government can do will either make life worse for everyone or if they try to be cautious about these problems, then they will effectively keep perpetuating the same problem endlessly.

Cyclical Changes in Nature

Modern thinking rests upon the idea of continuous progress,

linear time, and a world free of contradictions. Logic is free of contradictions; physics uses linear time; society progresses continuously. This is the dogma or doctrine under which every single subject operates. However, with this type of thinking, we can never understand or diagnose what is actually happening. For instance, if we had left behind feudalism, communism, and autocracy, and embraced free markets, capitalism, and democracy, then why is the past returning at present?

To understand these things, we have to rethink everything about logic, physics, and society we have thought of so far. One way to do that is to imagine the current economic state in terms of the yin-yang dynamic. It involves contradictions, cyclical time, and iterations.

In the yin-yang picture, there is a small black circle inside a white patch and a small white circle inside the black patch. Black and white are opposites, which we call "duality" in Vedic philosophy; they cannot exist on their own because they are defined by their opposites. These small black or white circles inside the bigger white or black patches are the in-built contradictions within each dualistic position.

For example, free-market capitalistic democracy was defined as the social opposition to feudalism, economic opposition to communism, and political opposition to autocracy. But most people did not understand that there is a seed of feudalism, communism, and autocracy built into corporations. A corporation is a feudal fiefdom in which the employees work for feudal lords—i.e., the upper echelons of corporate management—laboring for minimal wages while the feudal lords profit disproportionately from the work of a corporate employee. A corporation is communistic because the upper management has complete authority over the allocation of work, resources, and people, and the opinions of the employees do not matter; neither is the opinion ever solicited nor should it be given. A corporation is autocratic because anyone who shares their opinion, and questions the upper management or their policies, actions, or decisions is fired from the corporation.

This seed of autocracy, communism, and feudalism that exists inside corporations grows with the passing of time, until it swallows the free market, capitalism, and democracy, and undermines the basis on which such corporations were created. In the absence of this foundation, fewer new corporations are created, and even those are either absorbed into the same system or destroyed by current corporations.

In Vedic philosophy, we describe the process depicted in the yin-yang dynamic by the terms "dominant" and "subordinate". When democracy, free market, and capitalism are dominant, then autocracy, communism, and feudalism are subordinate. This subordinate entity is the small circle inside the dominant bigger patch. However, as time passes, the smaller circle grows in size and swallows the bigger patch, such that the small thing is now big, and the big thing is now small. The situation is now the opposite of what it was before.

The reversal of the dominant-subordinate positions creates a cycle of change in which history repeats itself. That is, even as something is subordinate right now, it exists as a small seed within the bigger thing, and it will be dominant in the future. Therefore, we might despair about the decline of society, economy, and politics in the short run, as we are effectively returning to the feudal, autocratic, and communistic past. But this too is not permanent. The situation will reverse again, which means that corporations will be destroyed from within.

Self-destruction can occur in many ways—(a) employees quit these corporations, (b) they divulge the corporate exploitative practices undermining the corporation's power, and (c) the selfish attitudes of the corporate leaders demotivate the employees and they stop working for the corporate interests. Basically, the destruction comes from within, and corporations will be undone by their members.

As this process of undermining from within begins, sometimes there are appearances of corrective actions to arrest the decline. But this is temporary and superficial. Corporate leaders, for instance, will often pretend to have become more democratic, and socialistic, or favor the free exchange of ideas and opinions. But that is a charade. Behind the superficial display of openness is the search for troublemakers to be rooted out and replaced by compliant and subservient employees who will toe the corporate line. The troublemakers will be fired from the corporation on whimsical grounds, or opportunistically as cost-reduction, resource redistribution, etc. The net effect of such a change is that the corporation's productivity, innovation, and zeal are destroyed. And that destruction results from the need to have complete power over the corporation. This desire grows with time, and therefore, once the process has begun, it has to go to its extreme and self-destruct.

Philosophical Implications

Dualism is often portrayed as the battle between opposites, but that is only half the story. The other half is an inner struggle between the opposing tendencies within, which produces an inner contradiction. The inner contradiction is the more important cause of change.

Due to these cycles of change, there is neither eternal hope nor eternal despair. Everything produces its own opposite because the seed of opposition exists within itself. This cyclical change is itself despair to the intelligent person because he can see that whatever good I'm doing now will be undone in the future. An intelligent person wishes to escape this cycle. The less intelligent people like to see progress and they despair lack of progress or temporary decline. The hopeful person suffers more than the hopeless person, and therefore hope is not a good thing. Hopeless existence is also not good. Only the escape from this cycle of endless change can be recommended.

Therefore, if you are despairing at the current predicament, then there is nothing to worry about because it will change eventually. Of course, you and I could be dead by then. By there is still nothing to worry about, as the soul which is not liberated from material existence, is reborn. So, you could be reborn to enjoy life again, temporarily. If you are thinking that change is always progress, then you will be disappointed.

Thus, it is said that the enlightened soul becomes detached from worldly events. He takes solace in devotion to the Lord and gives up the desire for materialistic progress. It is not that this progress never happens, but only that every progress is followed by a regress, and then again by progress. If you look long enough, then you can see why materialistic progress is futile. However, since people are so attached to this materialistic progress, therefore, we can spend time discussing the nature of this progress and describe why it is regressing rather than progressing. That may seem depressing to many people, but out of that despair can come detachment followed by enlightenment.

That enlightenment involves a *non-dualistic* reality in which the opposites are not separated and opposed to each other. Rather, they are combined in a way that despite the existence of variety, there is no contradiction between the varied things. When contradictions are resolved, then time becomes linear progress. And the world of conflicts is replaced by that of cooperation and mutual love.

Unless we understand how this world is dualistic, we cannot understand how the non-dualistic world is better, and why we should seek it. The discussion of this dualistic reality, the illustration of its problems, and the cause of those problems is also a useful topic if it illuminates the problems, detaches us from this world, impels us toward the search for another kind of reality, and explains both realities perfectly.

Why AI Is Deficient and Yet It Seems Very Powerful

In the previous article I discussed the implementation of AI and its use for controlling markets, governments, and people. In this post, I will do the opposite: Talk about why AI is deficient. To reconcile these two seemingly contradictory positions, we will then discuss how AI becomes powerful *if* society becomes homogeneous. The fact is that society has been progressively homogenizing through the spread of capitalism, democracy, industrialization, and globalization. This makes AI powerful because the diversity that complicates predictions is removed. In short, the technology of AI is useless unless the people in the society it controls are standardized to some specific norm.

Deficiencies of Artificial Intelligence

To understand the deficiencies in AI, one has to look at how it works on people. Most people are combinations of thousands of attributes, but for simplicity, I will use an example of two attributes.

Consider a person with two attributes— "rich" and "doctor". There are certain ways in which most rich people behave—they spend on expensive clothes, cars, houses, vacations, etc. And there are certain ways in which doctors behave—they care for patients, listen to their problems, and cure illnesses; they also go to medical conferences, read medical journals, and propose improvements in medicine.

The reality is that different people have these attributes in various *proportions*. In Vedic philosophy, we call these *dominant* and *subordinate*. For example, some rich doctors can have richness as the dominant attribute and doctorness as the subordinate attribute. Such a person will spend on flashy cars, houses, clothes, and vacations, and pay less attention to the condition of patients, the latest research in medicine, medical conferences, and so on. He will rather focus on the shortest path to make the most money because medicine is not itself the goal; it is only the route to becoming rich. Conversely, if a rich doctor has doctorness dominant and richness subordinate, then such a person will donate his riches to charity, lead a simple and frugal life, and spend time curing patients, understanding medicine, and trying to contribute to its progress. The riches of a doctor with doctorness prominent increase his focus on medicine and reduce it on richness. Conversely, the riches of a doctor with richness prominent decrease his focus on medicine and increase it on richness.

As you can see, modeling the real world is very hard—even with just two attributes—because they exist in dominant-subordinate states, which people will normally call various proportions. Even with minor changes to the dominant and subordinate state of an attribute, the behavior can change drastically. In reality, there are thousands of such attributes, which exist in different proportions, and modeling them into a trend is nearly impossible. Thereby, in Vedic philosophy, each person is unique, which means that there are thousands of attributes, and each person is a combination of some such attributes in different proportions or dominant and subordinate states.

Deficiencies of AI Training Methods

Now, the naïve person can argue: Even if there are infinite attributes, a computer system can still model them—uniquely for each person. Social media companies—as we discussed in the last post—are already trying to do that. But there is a problem: We don't have a *definition* of each attribute *a priori*.

For example, we don't know the meaning of the word "doctor" or "rich" *a priori*. This is because computers can never represent meaning. So, AI tries to substitute that meaning with *data*. This means that the word "rich" is defined by the behaviors of a collection of people. These people are collected into a group called "rich" by humans during the "training" phase of AI to produce a *model* of richness. For the computer, "rich" simply means a certain set of *behaviors,* and "richness" is the quality that produces that behavior. The problem is that richness as a quality can be present although it doesn't produce the behaviors of richness. The computer cannot understand or represent a quality that produces no effects because the quality is present only when the behavior is present. So, humans understand the quality, and computers collect the behaviors, and the human designates some behavior by some words such as "rich" or "doctor". The interface between humans and computers that maps a word to a behavior is called "training".

The problem with "training" is that there is no universal characterization of the presence of an attribute in terms of behavior. For example, when a rich doctor lives a frugal life, there is a contradiction in modeling: The person is rich, but he is not extravagant. So, should we model this guy as rich or poor? The intelligent human response would be: He is rich but that richness is subordinated. The artificial intelligence response would be that: He is not rich, because he is not exhibiting extravagance. A poor person is frugal because poverty is dominant, and a rich person is frugal because richness is subordinate. Since two opposite qualities—richness and poverty—can produce the same result of frugality, therefore, it is impossible to create a *qualitative understanding* of person-based behavioral modeling.

Philosophical Origins of AI Deficiencies

We can restate this problem in philosophical language: Knowing the cause fully determines the effect, however, knowing the effect is insufficient to determine the cause. In the words of Willard Quine, this is the problem of "underdetermination" in which the observation of effects underdetermines the cause. An example of this underdetermination is that frugal behavior can be caused both by poverty and richness. Likewise, even a poor person can borrow money from a bank, and exhibit richness for a short period of time. So, poverty and richness cannot be inferred from frugality and extravagance.

The net result of the problem of underdetermination is that we cannot "classify" a person correctly, and without classification, we cannot predict their behaviors. Whatever "typical" models we create based on a typical behavioral understanding of richness and poverty, will have many exceptions because there are so many atypical behaviors due to dominant-subordinate states, and those exceptions entail a failure in prediction, which then makes AI useless as it generates many false positives and false negatives.

The Role of Societal Diversity

However, the atypical cases are prominent only when society is *diverse* and qualities exist in various proportions or dominant-subordinate states. If society is homogenized, then there is a standard dominant-subordinate pattern of qualities. That homogenization means that all rich doctors will be extravagant, and all poor doctors will be frugal because the amount of wealth they have is *the* dominant determinant of their behavior. In short, to construct a model of behaviors, we must prior construct a standardized hierarchy of qualities—such as wealth is at the top, followed by looks and appearances, followed by a person's professional stature, followed by the work they do, etc.

Under this standardized model, rich and good-looking people will be always talking about their richness and good looks rather than discussing their profession, and those who don't flaunt their riches and looks and instead focus on their profession must be poor and ugly. If society can be standardized in such a model, then AI can become very successful, because now the atypical cases disappear from society. Everything neatly falls into a standard behavioral model, which makes predictions easy for an AI system.

The general principle of accurate predictions is that qualities fully determine behaviors, and when qualities exist in different dominant-subordinate states, then, behaviors cannot be reverse-engineered into qualities. However, if society is homogenized in terms of its qualities, then behavior can be reverse-engineered, encoded in a computer model, and predicted for any given input. In short, AI is successful when society is homogeneous, and unsuccessful when society is diverse. As people become standardized by the indoctrination of modern science, and the acceptance of a political, social, and economic ideology, it becomes easier to control them because they are now effectively like machines—standardized, replaceable, replicable, and uniform. A person is now effectively like a nut, bolt, or gear.

The Standardization of Humanity

Every totalitarian ruler dreams of standardized humans. This is the essence of the movie Matrix in which if you surrender your individuality to the "system", then the "system" rewards you. By that reward, the "system" tells you how a human has to behave. If you deviate from a set behavior, then the "system" punishes you. By that punishment, the "system" tells you how a human should not behave.

Over time, through rewards and punishments, you *train* a person to become a standardized nut, bolt, or gear. Standardization is the preliminary step toward social control. Non-standardized humans cannot be controlled easily. And standardized humans can be controlled very easily. So, as humans conform to some expected norms of behavior, they become easily controllable.

All large modern societies try to produce standardized humans by indoctrinating them through education, television, political and economic policies, and socially acceptable norms. The AI system can do the same. Even if it cannot gain a good understanding of a person, it can still "train" them by injecting moods, ideas, and judgments by showing them some images, news articles, and role models. As a person is repeatedly exposed to certain types of images, news articles, and role models he or she starts becoming standardized.

For example, if women wearing certain types of clothes are promoted and popularized as the de-facto standard of beauty, then most women will gradually accept that standard. They will feel guilty about the absence of such clothes and try to model themselves after the advertised standard. Likewise, if certain types of language, ideas, and beliefs are discouraged, then people accept them as standards and begin conforming. Thereby, a standardized human is produced in society.

We don't even have to know what humans are, to begin with. Instead, we can conjure a predefined image of the human and feed it repeatedly to them. Over time, they will become the thing they see. Then we already know what they are, and we can control them accordingly.

Standardization Overcomes Flaws of AI

Therefore, AI has fatal flaws if we think of it as modeling reality, because it cannot correctly model diversity, the understanding of qualities, and the prediction of behaviors based on qualities. However, AI is very powerful, if it is used to indoctrinate people to create a standardized human. The flaws of AI are relevant only if the reality is diverse. If diversity is destroyed by indoctrination, then that standardized nut, bolt, or gear would be easily modeled by AI, giving the AI system control over people's lives.

Therefore, the flaws of AI can be overcome through systematic indoctrination, enforcement of politically correct behaviors, homogenization of society, and the destruction of ideological and cultural diversity. In one sense, the brouhaha about the power of AI is misleading. In another sense, it is a scary truth. AI is powerless in the face of diversity. And yet, it gains power through the standardization of humans.

The technology giants, and the experts in AI, understand these things but ordinary people don't. And because they don't understand the flaws of AI, and how it can gain power via standardization, they fail to see why AI technology giants are so enmeshed with a certain definition of a standardized human. They know the flaws of AI, and they know that to improve it, humans have to be standardized.

How Tech Companies Push Social Standardization

In the US, for example, AI is done in Silicon Valley companies, and they have a premeditated idea about a standardized human. This human works for long hours, eats food by calorific value divided into proteins, carbohydrates, proteins, and fats, is polite toward other people, upholds gender equality, respects other races, religions, and countries, favors democracy and capitalism over other systems, believes in college education as the road to a happy life, is prepared to take large debts in order to finance his education, house, and car, and invests most of their earning through the stock market in other technology companies that advance this agenda (preferably AI itself).

With this premeditated idea of a standardized human, Silicon Valley companies finance, promote, and advocate a norm of humanity to the rest of the world. As technology permeates, society gets more standardized, which gives Silicon Valley companies the power to control and predict their behaviors better and push for more standardization of education, culture, politics, economics, and social norms, which then further increases their power to push even more standardization. In short, by indoctrination, a standardized human is created, which gives AI the power to predict and control, which perpetuates the cycle of indoctrination, standardization, and increasing control.

This is a journey in which one starts from a position of weakness but gains immense power over time. Paying people high salaries if they conform to a predefined standardized norm is part of that process—it is a reward system that works for you if you accept the definition of a standardized human and advance it. Thereby, technology direction is deeply enmeshed with a social, economic, political, cultural, and scientific ideology, because those at the helm of these technology companies know that their future power rests on today's indoctrination.

Just like nuts and bolts have standard sizes, are mass-produced, and easily fitted in many types of machines, similarly, if humans can be standardized then they can be mass-produced and easily moved from one corporation, society, or country to another. This ability of a nut or bolt to fit into different kinds of machines is a "freedom" and its counterpart in society is that people can move from one corporation, society, or country to another. Thus, technology companies talk about freedom, but it is not the freedom that you and I normally imagine—i.e., to be what we want to be, to choose our lifestyle, ideals, values, and worldviews. It is rather the freedom to move within a system governed by some standards. Therefore, the discourse on "freedom" and "liberty" is highly misleading, because there are two radically different ideas about freedom: The freedom to move a nut or bolt from one machine to another vs. the freedom to be what you want to be.

The Progress of Industrialization

This trend, however, is not new. At the dawn of industrialization, people had to be fitted into factories, working on standard hours, doing standardized jobs, governed by a system of standardized rules and processes, being paid standard salaries, dressed in standardized attire, and conforming to a standardized way of talking. This standardization then progressed into what a person learned in school, how he or she was tested by standardized examinations, and how a person had to master a standardized textbook in order to succeed in examinations. This process then deepened into a definition of social norms where a person had to have a house in a certain type of locality, was measured by the title in the company he or she worked for, had to buy all their things from some standardized outlets, which placed their products in some standardized fashion. It then progressed into the standardization of what types of ideas are acceptable in academia, what political views were acceptable for politicians, and what economic policies had to be followed lest there be retaliation from the powerful forces.

Industrialization means standardization. As time passes, people conform to more and more standards, and because society has become homogenized due to the proliferation of standard scientific theories, and economic, political, and sociological norms, that we can even imagine the potential of AI to control people.

Even then, AI is not that powerful, unless people are further standardized. Therefore, AI is the next step in industrialization, which means the standardization of personal preferences, values, and moral systems, and the adoption of standard forms of ethical behavior. Greater industrialization entails greater standardization, greater totalitarian control, and greater loss of freedom to be what you want to be. A person is standardized by a system of rewards (if you conform to the standard) and punishments (if you deviate from the standardized idea of humans). Ultimately, humans are also machines in an industrialized society. And because this idea is not new, and has been progressing gradually, by the time excessive control of society arrives under technology's control, people will accept it just as they have in the past.

It is just like how industrial workers accepted standardization in factories, education, and social, economic, and political thinking. Until that goal is achieved, advocates of AI will talk about how technological progress made society better in the past, and how prosperity followed a new phase of industrialization, while never talking about how each individual is becoming a mechanized cog in a larger machine.

Industrialization Ends People's Freedoms

A machine has no choice; it does what its owner wants it to do. Likewise, as humans become standardized, they become mechanized, and they lose control over their lives. They are owned by a person who owns a gigantic machine, and the essence of humanity—i.e., freedom and choice—is destroyed. You lose the idea that you have a purpose in life, that you can choose a purpose, and lead the life that you want, because you are indoctrinated by education in school, by media in your free time, by a corporation while you are working, and by the pressure to conform by your friends and family who are in turn buying into predefined ideas of humanity through advertisements. The economic rewards you receive are in return for surrendering your freedom, time, and priorities.

The difference is simply that as industrialization progresses, it encroaches upon deeper and deeper aspects of a person. Initially, when workers work in a factory, industrialization only gets to control their bodies. Then, as industrial education, it takes control of your mind. By encroaching economy, society, and politics, it dictates your self-beliefs. Then, it takes hold of your goals by telling you what is respectable and lovable in an industrial society. Then, it takes control of your moral virtues or what you consider morally right and wrong. Finally, you lose every kind of choice that made you distinctly you.

These invasions and intrusions of industrialization are spiritually devastating in the sense that people stop believing that they have a *choice*. With the death of choice, dies the idea that there is a soul. With that, dies the idea that there is a world beyond this world. And with the death of transcendence, dies the idea of God, and a relationship between soul and God. Society now becomes atheistic, simply because you were standardized by indoctrination.

AI is just the next step in this spiritual destruction. It is not a new thing; it is a progression of a trend that began with industrialization. The novelty is that it is deepening the control of humanity, reducing their choices, and standardizing their likes and dislikes, cultures, and political, economic, social, and scientific ideologies. Therefore, there are no "good" vs. "bad" AI. It is all bad because when it progresses, humanity is standardized, freedoms are lost, and people lose the sense of choice and spirituality. That spiritual decline outstrips whatever material benefits may accrue temporarily. And it progresses because people don't have a spiritual vision for themselves. So, they prioritize the material benefits over spiritual well-being and let industrialization gain increasing control over their present lives.

The Role of Spiritual Education

This is where spiritual education is important: It tells us that we have a *choice*, that we are spiritual beings, and that despite what our employer, family, friends, and education tell us, we can reject these things. Of course, such rejection is very hard, because, with the passing of time, the pressure is constantly mounting. The more we succumb to pressures, the more we will lose the willpower to resist them in the future.

The discussion of the flaws of AI is a stepping stone in this direction because we can see that machines don't have the capacity to process meaning or choices, and they are powerless in the face of diverse humanity. A machine should never be able to control a human. However, the machine gains this control if we become standardized to behave in some predefined ways. The power of AI is the result of the power that we have gradually and progressively surrendered via industrialization. If we want to take back that power, then we have to reject the indoctrination and even though it seems hard, the rejection is not whimsical or irrational. It is founded on a scientific understanding of the body, mind, and soul, how the soul is trapped in the body and mind, and how by progressively controlling the body followed by the mind, a machine can gain complete control over the soul.

The best day to begin spiritual education was yesterday. The next best day is today. As time passes, the will to reject the indoctrination decreases, and surrendering to external control seems a more comfortable alternative. Thus, things will not be easier tomorrow than they are today. They will be harder. This should be a wake-up call to anyone who wants to push this problem to the future. The system may or may not change, but you can change by seeing its flaws, rejecting the system, and protecting yourself from its invasive techniques. That ability to separate oneself from the system itself requires detachment, which is a reflection of a choice, which is a symptom of the soul.

The choice of the soul is simply attachment and detachment. When we attach ourselves to something, we surrender our freedom. When we detach ourselves from it, we regain our freedom. Ultimately, we cannot remain detached and we have to attach ourselves to something. That means surrendering our freedom to be controlled by someone. Who is that someone? It could be a person who wants to love us or a person who wants to use us. Since we can choose where we attach, therefore, we have a choice. Since we can choose better and worse points of attachment, therefore, there are better and worse choices. That choice is never lost. But a person who is attached to one thing may take time to detach himself or herself from it and attach it to something else and until that shift occurs it seems we don't have a choice.

How Descartes Created Science from Religion

How Descartes Came to Philosophize

It is commonly believed that Descartes was the first modern philosopher, but the fact is that philosophy was an afterthought for Descartes. His initial work was on *analytical geometry*, which created a relation between geometry and algebra through the use of a coordinate system.

Descartes intended to construct a "physics" from it—a rational and empirical description of the world. However, when this manuscript was about to be published, Descartes heard about Galileo's Inquisition for advocating a rational and empirical study of the world, instead of relying on the Church and the Bible. Realizing that he would meet the same fate as Galileo if his mathematical work was published, Descartes withdrew his work on analytical geometry, and went about writing a philosophical defense of a rational and empirical study of the world.

This work, which he called "Meditations", was dedicated to "The Most Wise and Illustrious Doctors of the Sacred Faculty of Theology in Paris" for obvious reasons. However, this philosophical defense of a rational and empirical science was deceptive because Descartes wrote to this friend "... the six Meditations contain all the fundamental ideas of my physics. But please keep this quiet." This article explores the structure of this deceptive argument.

The Structure of the Cartesian Argument

The argument by Descartes can be summarized into the following steps:

1. I cannot trust my senses and my mind to know the world with certainty. This was also the argument of the Church, and it concluded that the world had to be known through the scripture because the revealed scripture was not based on discoveries of the senses and the mind.

2. However, I don't need the certainty of the senses and the mind to know that I exist; I can know my existence with certainty from the fact of the existence of any sensation and thought. This is the well-known Cartesian dictum *cogito ergo sum* or that "I think therefore I exist".

3. Once the self is established beyond doubt, we can analyze our minds, and we find that it contains *innate ideas* such as a "perfect being", "substance", "self", etc. These ideas are not obtained by the analysis of the external world, and therefore they are innate ideas.

4. Just as the sum of all angles of a triangle equals 180° is part of the idea of a triangle, similarly, the *existence* of a perfect being is a part of the idea of a "perfect being". Just as the truth of the sum of angles is guaranteed whenever we speak of a triangle, similarly, the existence of a perfect being is guaranteed whenever we speak about the "perfect being".

5. This perfect being will not allow our minds to be deceived by an evil genius, which means that if we see an external world, then there must really be an external world. However, since we sometimes have hallucinations, therefore, the real external world could not be how we see it. Rather, the world must be analytical geometry that is not subject to hallucinations.

6. To the extent that we can use our minds to understand geometry, and we can use our senses to realize the presence of geometrical truth in the external world, our senses and the mind are useful sources of knowledge about the real world, and they can be trusted to know.

Without getting into the merits of the argument, we can look at its *structure*. The argument begins by saying that "I cannot trust my senses and the mind" and concludes by saying that "I can trust my senses and the mind". Whatever else is said in between the premise and the conclusion doesn't matter, because the two are logically contradictory. A valid argument should not have such a contradiction. But if that contradiction has appeared, then there is something wrong with the argument. We can now focus on finding that flaw.

But before that, let's address the objection from *reductio ad absurdum* or the proof by contradiction. In a proof by contradiction, we use a premise to arrive at a conclusion that is either manifestly absurd or contradicts another established fact. By the absurdity of the conclusion, or the contradiction to another established fact, the starting premise is disproven and is thereby rejected. In the case of the Cartesian argument, the starting premise is that we cannot trust our senses, and the conclusion is that we can. For *reductio* to apply, we must say that the conclusion that we can trust our senses must be absurd or contradictory to other facts, and thereby, we can reject the premise that the senses cannot be trusted. In short, we must reject the idea that senses can be trusted to prove that the senses can be trusted. This, as we can see, is not a valid reductio because X must be false to say that X is true.

The point is that proof by contradiction doesn't apply to self-contradiction between premise and conclusion. Descartes uses a self-contradictory structure and presents it as a legitimate argument.

The Flaw in the Cartesian Argument

But where is the flaw in the argument? Is the idea that we know our own existence with certainty flawed? No, that is not a flaw; we do know our existence for sure. Then, is the existence of innate ideas such as "perfect being" flawed? At least in Vedic philosophy, everything you can imagine can also exist in reality, although it might exist temporarily. The question is: Can perfection be eternal? The answer is yes, although this is not innately known by everyone. Many cynical people might say: There is no such thing as perfection or idealism. American Pragmatism, for instance, began by rejecting the pursuit of perfection and ideals, and substituting it with "whatever works for the time being". Clearly, the claim that perfection is known by everyone innately is false, although perfection itself is not false. Since perfection itself is not false, what we derive by that assumption is also not going to be false. Therefore, even this supposition will not lead to a false conclusion, although it can be disputed by many.

Then, the Ontological Argument, that existence is innate to the idea of perfection is not false, because every idea can exist, although temporarily. So, even if we have a subjective notion of perfection, that idea can also exist temporarily. The question is again: Can this existence be eternal? And that depends on how perfect is our perfect. Assuming that our perfect is truly perfect, it can be eternally real. So, the Ontological Argument that embeds reality into the idea of perfection is also not a flawed idea.

Now, comes the problematic part of the argument, namely, that the perfect being will not deceive us. This is certainly false in Vedic philosophy because the world is said to be delusionary in the sense that we can have false ideas about it. Such false theories are also temporary, even as those ideas exist as a possibility eternally. Their realization always requires an individual, and the association of the individual with that idea is temporary and hence false. For example, the idea "father" is eternal, but "I am a father" is temporary and false. Likewise, the idea "man" is eternal, but "I am a man" is temporary and false. Since we believe in all such ideas, therefore, we are factually under a delusion. And the material world exists precisely to create such delusions *because we want to be deluded in many ways.*

The claim that God will not delude us is valid if we don't want to be deluded. But that claim is false if we desire to prove that we are great, invincible, powerful, etc.—which are all delusional desires. Thereby, a worldly delusion is created by God to help us enjoy such fantasies temporarily. Since God creates that temporary delusion for us to fulfill our fantasies, therefore, God is also deluding us.

Thus, the material world is a delusion, because God is deluding us. After all, we want to enjoy false fantasies. Since God is deluding us to fulfill our desires for delusion, therefore, neither our minds nor our senses are perfect sources of truth. To obtain that truth, we have to remove our desire for delusion. Then, God can remove the delusionary experiences, and reveal the truth to us, and then, the senses and the mind become sources of perfect knowledge. Until then, the senses and the mind are delusionary.

Therefore, the flaw in the Cartesian argument is that God does not delude us. In Vedic philosophy, God is also an evil genius, and He exhibits that evil ingenuity to cure us of the evil in us. In simple words, He creates the delusion of our invincibility and then destroys our power. He can create the illusion of knowledge, and then later on we realize that was we thought was knowledge was actually ignorance.

The idea of the "perfect being" in Cartesian philosophy suffers from the problem of evil in Christianity. If God is good, then how can evil exist in the world? And the answer is that God is both good and evil. If we are good, then God exhibits the good side, and if we are evil, then God exhibits the evil side. Thereby, good and evil are aspects of God. However, since God is always good in Christianity, therefore, Christian priests could not question this idea for the same reason that they could not explain the origin of evil.

In one sense, their idea of a "perfect being" is not so perfect. And that imperfection in their idea of a "perfect being" allowed Descartes to claim that God would never delude us. If we take out that claim, then the conclusion that we can trust our senses and mind would also not exist. Thereby, the whole argument about the validity of reason and experience to study the world would collapse.

In one sense, we can say that the imperfect idea of God, which rationalizes knowledge via senses and the mind, is the cause of modern science. That idea also leads to the problem of evil. And if the problem of evil is solved, then the Cartesian foundation of science disappears. Of course, Christian priests could not fault Descartes for saying that God is good, so they had to accept the Cartesian argument. And that argument introduced the validity of mental reason and sense experience to create modern science.

The Vedic Argument for Reason and Experience

Now, you might assume that if we acknowledge God's perfection, then we would have to reject reason and experience as methods of knowledge. But that is not true because reason and experience are also methods to know the good, to distinguish the good from evil, just as they are the methods to conflate evil with good. Our minds and senses can be deluded, or they can reveal the truth. Everything depends on our attitude. If our attitude is good, then reason and experience are valid methods to know the truth. If the attitude is evil, then reason and experience are delusionary.

Therefore, scriptures are prescribed as a method to fix our attitude, but the truth of the scripture is not contrary to reason and experience. If we fix our attitude according to the scripture, then the truth stated in the scripture can also be confirmed by reason and experience. Some reasoning and experience are required to read the scripture, analyze its teachings, and practice its instructions. If all reason and experience were flawed, then we would be deluded even while reading the scripture. Therefore, reason and experience cannot be *in principle* rejected. They have to be rejected based on our attitudes.

Thereby, the rejection of the Cartesian argument doesn't mean blind faith in the scripture or even the blanket rejection of reason and experience. There can be eternal scientific truth—confirmed by reason and experience—that is identical to that in scripture. And there can be some temporary and imperfect scientific truth—confirmed by reason and experience—that is contrary to the scripture.

The reality is that when Descartes established the validity of the scientific method, he used the existence of God as the lever to solve the problem of hallucination, misperception, and an evil genius deluding our minds. This lever then justified the use of reason and experience to study the world. However, because there were no caveats to the use of reason and experience, therefore, when science rejected God's existence, another self-contradiction between premise and conclusion was created. The new problem for Christianity is that if we say that God deludes us, then we cannot use reason and experience, and religion becomes blind faith. But if we say that God doesn't delude us, then we can use reason and experience to reject God, and the situation worsens—religion is still blind faith, plus it is irrational and unempirical.

Therefore, the idea that God is both good and evil, and He reveals one side to us based on our attitude is essential to (a) religion being accessible through scriptures, (b) religion being confirmable through reason and experience, and (c) science confirming the same truth as accessible via religion.

Hidden Attitudes in the Cartesian Argument

The Cartesian argument is clever, and it exploits a weakness in Christianity: It uses the Christian idea of God to promulgate an ideology that over time undermines Christianity. This, as I noted at the start, was the purpose behind the Cartesian argument. Catholic priests failed to see what Descartes was actually doing. Blinded by the deceptive dedication and praise to God, they were easily deceived.

One unmissable aspect of Cartesian metaphysics is the use of only two substances—mind and matter—leaving God out of the ontology completely. Obviously, God cannot be matter, because matter is inert. And God cannot be the mind, because then everyone in the world would become God. You need a third category—a *res theos* apart from *res extensa* and *res cogitans*—to acknowledge that God is real. But Descartes did not induct this category. He opportunistically used the Ontological Argument to say that God must be real because it was necessary to overcome the problem of "senses and mind cannot be trusted". But once he established the reality of the mind and the world using that argument, he discarded God. Thereby, Cartesian metaphysics only recognizes mind and body and not God.

Cartesian metaphysics was prescient: The subsequent development of science followed the same trajectory, namely, mind and body are ontologically real, but God has no ontological reality. Over time, you can also say that since mind-body dualism is problematic, therefore, there is no mind apart from the body. Thus, initially, you reduce three categories—God, mind, and body—into two: mind and body. Then you reduce these two further into one—body. And now everything becomes materialism.

In contrast, in Vedic philosophy, God, matter, and soul are always three distinct categories. Thereby, any attempts to reduce these three categories to fewer categories are rejected. For example, impersonalism tries to reduce God, soul, and matter to just God and matter, and that is rejected. Likewise, voidism tries to reduce soul, God, and matter to just matter, and that too is rejected. And since you cannot reduce three categories to fewer categories, therefore, the result of interactions between these categories creates even more categories. For instance, the interaction between soul and matter creates karma and the soul is bound to matter by karma. Likewise, the interaction between God and matter requires Causal Time, to transform His eternal will to purify the soul into a temporal manifestation of the will's fulfillment. However, if God and soul are removed, then Eternal Time and karma are also removed as a result. Then, we are left only with matter, and that is indeed the state of modern science.

The Creation of Science from Religion

The essence of the Cartesian argument is that of *using* God to get the entitlement to study the material world by our senses and the mind, and derecognizing God once that entitlement is obtained.

Now, Christians can gloat over the fact that science was created from Christianity because that is indeed true. And scientists can reject Christianity because that's what Descartes was actually doing. Since both claims are based on the same argument, therefore, they are merely two sides of the same coin.

To overcome this science-religion dichotomy, we have to realize that the Cartesian argument is flawed. It rests on a false idea of God, as someone who is only good; in fact, God in this false conception is so good, that He permits the soul to study the world only to be rejected by that study. This so-called "goodness" in God makes God so helpless that He has effectively been deceived by a carefully designed Ontological Argument. If God is so weak, then naturally, the power of God is transferred to the soul. Now, theologians may make further changes to extend the soul's power, thereby further weakening God's position. For example, some religious theologies postulate that each soul can draw up a personal contract with God, that God has no power to reject whereas the soul has the full power to change. As these contracts become more self-serving, rather than God-serving, the difference between religion and atheism keeps narrowing.

If we had any idea of how great God is, how magnificent His power is, and how His deluding energy is enslaving the soul through the body, senses, and the mind, then we would not think in this way.

Thus, both atheism and religion have become different aspects of a weakening position of God and strengthening the position of the individual in this world. The religion may recognize a weak God and atheism may reject His existence. Those acceptances and rejections are equally false and frivolous.

Scientific Pretensions of Evolutionary Theory

There is a difference between *evolution* and the *theory of evolution*. It's the same difference as that between planetary motion and Newton's theory of planetary motion. This distinction appears as that between *facts* and *truths*. They are not the same thing. Evolution is a fact, but the theory of evolution can be true or false. Likewise, planetary motion is a fact, but Newton's theory of planetary motion can be true or false. So, the factual existence of evolution doesn't guarantee the truth of the theory of evolution. We can determine the facts of evolution by observations, such as fossil records. But that doesn't mean the theory of evolution is true. Most people don't get the distinction between fact and truth. So, they equate the facts of evolution with the truth of the theory of evolution. They are not the same.

So, given that evolution is a fact, what makes a theory of evolution true? A theory is necessarily defined by two characteristics—explanation and prediction. A theory that explains but cannot predict, or a theory that predicts but cannot explain, is not a theory. This post discusses these issues.

Peg and Hole Methodology

Evolutionary theory can be simply stated as the model in which there is a hole called the "environment" into which a species adapts like a peg. Basically, some pegs have to fit into some holes. If the pegs don't conform to the holes, then one of two things can happen: (a) the hole changes to conform to the shape of the peg, and (b) the peg changes to conform to the shape of the whole. That is *adaptation*.

However, we don't know which of these two will happen, which is indeterminism. The peg can change the shape of the hole, or the hole can change the shape of the peg. The practical application of this in the context of evolution is that a change in the species can change the environment, or a change in an environment can change the species. The results in these two cases will be identical, which means that you cannot tell whether the change in species changed the environment or vice versa.

Indeterminism results from this inability—it is the inability to *explain* the outcomes *post facto*. Which means that if we observe some fossils, were they caused by a change in species, or a change in the environment? Since both causes result in the same outcome, therefore, there is no *necessity* in causation. You can still say that since either of these changes could have caused it, therefore, both causes are *sufficient*. A cause that is sufficient but not necessary is not the *true cause*. It is just a potential cause, but something has to activate one of the potentials into a true cause. If we cannot explain that potential, then it is as good as saying that there are just potentials but no reality.

Indeterminism in Newton's Physics

This problem of indeterminism, which results from the absence of *necessity,* was first highlighted by David Hume. But, of course, he was ignored. The problem then reappeared in Newton's mechanics.

For instance, when two particles collide, they can merge or split. You can imagine a car crashing into a truck. How a car splits into pieces is unpredictable—the total weight, speed, and all other properties collectively cannot determine how the car crash will split the car into pieces. Then, you can also have a truck crash into a car, which would constitute an alternative explanation of the same outcome.

Since the crash can be caused either by a car ramming a truck or a truck ramming a car, therefore, there is no fixed explanation. Similarly, the outcome of that crash—i.e., how the car splits into pieces—is also unpredictable in mechanics. Thereby, there is no fixed explanation and there is no fixed prediction.

David Hume's argument on necessity simplified the problem by saying that two fixed particles are colliding, which is like saying that a specific car crashes into a specific truck. Since we cannot predict the outcome of the crash, therefore, there is no predictive certainty and hence indeterminism. However, that is not the only type of uncertainty. It is also possible that the car crashes into a different truck, producing the same outcome. That would also deprive us of explanatory certainty.

The classical mechanical counterpart of this problem would be to substitute one of the colliding particles with another *identical* particle—i.e., that has the same mass, energy, momentum, angular momentum, etc. Even if the outcome is the same, you still have uncertainty: You don't know *which* particles caused the outcome. That uncertainty is however an explanatory rather than predictive uncertainty.

When we put these two types of uncertainties together, then we find that Newton's mechanics is both predictively and explanatorily uncertain. That uncertainty doesn't impact celestial mechanics because planets are not colliding. So, you create the semblance of a deterministic theory, by choosing a specific type of phenomenon where its problems are not exposed. Similarly, when we apply Newton's mechanics to the terrestrial mechanics, we choose those phenomena where objects don't merge and split. For instance, when a bat hits a ball, the bat and ball do not merge and split. Also, you assume that there is always one bat and one ball. If players use a different bat or a different ball, to score the same number of runs, then the explanation of runs would be indeterministic as the bat and ball are not fixed.

In short, the most deterministic theory in physics is indeterministic. It actually has no predictive or explanatory power, and it is hence not a theory. And yet, you can create the illusion of a theory by limiting its application to non-colliding planets, or a colliding bat and ball that do not split or merge.

Indeterminism in Evolutionary Theory

The same indeterminism exists even in evolutionary theory. Species and their environment are not like non-colliding planets;

they are also not like a bat and ball that do not split or merge on their collision. They are like a truck and car that collide and the result is completely unpredictable. Even which species will be changed by interaction to which part of the environment is inexplicable because different factors in the environment can produce the same outcomes. That is like a car colliding with a different truck.

Evolutionary theory is as indeterministic as Newton's mechanics. But the indeterminism in Newton's mechanics is *hidden* in celestial mechanics because planets don't collide, and it is *hidden* in terrestrial mechanics if we apply its principles to those collisions that don't merge or split the particles. Since these two principles don't apply to biological systems, therefore, all the weaknesses of Newton's mechanics must be visible. And that visibility entails that there is neither predictive nor explanatory power.

In simple words, given the situation today, there is no amount of computational power that can predict the future species, because it is entirely contingent on what happens on a collision of particles in a species with the particles in the environment, and the outcomes are never predictable. If we cannot predict the outcome of a single collision, then the split or merged particles resulting from that collision will produce even more uncertainty because they can now collide with different particles in different species or in different parts of the environment. The result is that the uncertainty must *explode* with passing time. That explosion means that the more you go into the future, the less you can predict. You have much better chances of predicting exactly what will happen tomorrow, and those chances keep declining *exponentially* with passing time. That destroys any hope of any kind of prediction.

Similarly, given the fossil data *post facto*, there is no amount of computational power that can explain what happened in the past, which then led to the current situation of species distribution.

The problem of predicting the future or explaining the past is not about the limits of computational power. It is not about the enormous number of equations that may be involved in this computation. It is not about the fact that we might not be able to collect all the data to make that computation. The issue is that even if we had infinite computational power, that could compute infinite equations, fueled by all the possible data, it would still be impossible to make a prediction of the future or explain the past.

The issue is that the theories are *mathematically* indeterministic. And the evolutionary theory is as indeterministic as Newton's mechanics. Therefore, we don't need to use a single fact from biology to explain why evolutionary theory is not a scientific theory. We can know that from physics itself.

The reason this equivalence between Newton's mechanics and evolutionary theory is not obvious to most people is that Newton's mechanics is applied to celestial and terrestrial mechanics in a way that hides its problems: Either the bodies don't collide, or they don't split and merge in a collision. If we take that assumption away, then all the flaws of Newton's mechanics exist in evolutionary theory.

The Problem of Evolutionary Discontinuity

The situation gets even worse as we add *constraints* to a biological system. For example, if we say that an ecosystem of species is a *closed system*, then such closed systems can only exist in mutually orthogonal *normal modes*. You can imagine a drum. Depending on where the drum is hit on the surface, it will always produce a specific sound, which is the sound of the drum as a whole. We cannot have individual parts of the drum vibrate in different ways individually—because the parts of the drum are tightly interconnected. The drum can only shift from one vibrational state to another, which are called the normal modes of the drum. This means that if a biological system is a closed ecosystem, then no individual species can evolve *individually*. Either the entire ecosystem evolves from one state to another, or the ecosystem will be in a fixed state. That collective ecosystem change requires an external event, quite like someone hitting the surface of the drum—to change the entire ecosystem at once. Thereby, incremental mutations that incrementally lead to bigger changes are impossible in a closed system.

Then, if we say that the biological system is not completely closed, but somewhat porous, then all the changes in the ecosystem will dissipate over time such that even if a species evolved to a new state in the ecosystem, that change will dissipate outward returning the ecosystem to its original state. Thereby, one should see a species X evolve to Y and then evolve back to X. That will make evolution reversible.

The problems get worse when we replace classical mechanics with quantum mechanics. Now, there is an ecosystem, which can be *represented* through many *orthogonal bases* quite like the orthogonal normal modes of classical mechanics. The difference is simply that all the components of the basis—i.e., the species of the ecosystem—are not simultaneously observable. So, you see species manifest one after another and even as the other species are invisible, they are still playing a role in the ecosystem.

These missing species are just like people in a team who have gone on vacation. The team operates sub-optimally without all its team members, but each member does things that they are designated to do *as if* all the team members are present. So, you get a fossil record at one time—like a team photo with some team members on vacation—and you think that it is the true ecosystem, but it is not. Then you take the next fossil record with a different set of team members on vacation, and you get a completely different picture. You think that the team is evolving when it is people going on vacations.

Then, the problem gets even more complicated if a quantum system shifts from one basis to another, which is achieved in a slit experiment by changing the number of slits—i.e., something outside the ecosystem. You take one fossil record, and you get a set of species {X}. And you take another fossil record, and you get a completely different set of species {Y}, and you think that the ecosystem is evolving. But it is the same ecosystem, which has jumped from one species-set to another due to an external change. If we combine the basis change with the occasional visibility of the basis components, then the situation is akin to people in a team reorganizing themselves frequently—i.e., doing different jobs—along with some team members going on vacations. Now, the periodic snapshots of the team are even more misleading because the team members are evolving to play different roles *and* going on vacations.

As you can tell, we don't need any biology to understand these problems. We just need to know a little bit about physics and the mathematics that underlies that physics. It is not even rigorous physics and mathematics; just the high-level descriptions of (a) closed systems interacting with other systems like a hand hitting a drum, (b) semi-porous systems that dissipate changes outwardly like a loosely tied drum, and (c) quantum systems that shift from one basis to another, and (d) components of those bases are observed occasionally.

All these problems make the proposition of evolutionary explanation much harder. A small external intervention like a hand hitting a drum can change the entire ecosystem, with all the species evolving suddenly and collectively, not incrementally through random mutation and adaptation. Then, evolutionary changes can become reversible if the system is semi-porous or dissipative. Then, fossil records are simply snapshots of a team with some members missing, so you cannot say that species are evolving even though some members appear and disappear from the fossil record. Then, the entire ecosystem can jump from one set of species to another, and while you are drawing a diagram of continuity in evolution, all you see is discontinuity which you can never explain correctly.

Summarizing the Problems

Even if we just extend the classical mechanical model of nature to biological systems, there is still no prediction and explanation, although there is *continuity,* which means that there is an incremental succession of states. That succession of states can translate into continuous changes in fossil records, which we can collect, although we can never explain that succession using a formal theory because the classical physical explanatory model is indeterministic in both predictions and explanations.

Then, if we say that the ecosystem is closed, semi-porous, or quantum mechanical, then new problems of *discontinuity* arise, in which changes are sudden and inexplicable, and the problem of determinism still exists. That means, you collect fossil records, and you will see numerous discontinuities. However, you can never explain what is causing that discontinuity because you are always thinking that species cannot appear and disappear, that if some change in species has occurred then it will not be reversed, and that all changes in species are incremental and slow rather than sudden, disruptive, and pervasive.

The persistent fact about evolutionary fossil records is discontinuity. However, this discontinuity is generally rubbished in modern biology as missing intermediate fossil records. The evolutionist says: If only we had all the fossil records, then we will know that the evolution is not discontinuous. But that is something the evolutionist can never achieve—isn't it? There will never be enough fossil evidence to certify incremental observation, in order for the continuity to be established and discontinuity to be ruled out. The limits of fossil collection themselves play into the hands of the evolutionist who insists on continuity, rules out discontinuity as an aberration caused by inadequate fossil records, to be overcome by the discovery of fossils in the *future*. That future, as we know quite well, will never arrive.

On the contrary, there exists clear evidence of discontinuous changes such as in the Cambrian Explosion, and these discontinuities are not the only ones. Faced with such problems, biologists offer excuses: "Well, discontinuous changes don't undermine the fundamental thesis of evolution, namely, that we evolved from a common ancestor". That is as lame as saying that all shirts, pants, blouses, and skirts evolved from primordial deerskin. Or, that all the books in all the libraries of the world evolved from a common book. Just because they appear one after another doesn't mean they incrementally *evolved* from the previous thing. Making that assertion needs proof for continuity, which as we saw above, isn't there. In fact, all the data we have is highly discontinuous. Furthermore, even if you insist that they have evolved through continuous and incremental changes, you still need to present a *causal model* of that change, and then employ it to predict future evolutions. Until you can predict and explain—without mathematical indeterminism in the theory—you don't have a theory of evolution.

Modern Biology is Not a Unique Science

Biology can differ from physics in *facts*, but it cannot differ from physics in *truths*. This is not *my* claim but the claim of biologists themselves, because they reduce all biology to chemistry, all chemistry is then reduced to quantum mechanics. The truths of biology and physics now involve the same fundamental principles of space, time, causation, and change, which have to be complete in their predictions and explanations, and they have to be proven to be necessary and sufficient. Similarly, such theories have to employ a model of discontinuous change if we treat the universe quantum mechanically, or continuity if we think that quantum discontinuity reduces to classical continuity.

If someone believes that quantum discontinuities reduce to classical continuity, then we already know that classical mechanics is indeterministic, which means that we will never get a theory of evolution by such reduction. As we have seen, all such theories appear to be predictively complete only in so far as objects do not collide, or if the object collision doesn't cause object merger or splitting.

If instead someone wishes to treat the universe quantum mechanically, then they better find a complete model of predictions and explanations, which is also necessary and sufficient, in quantum mechanics—before they talk about the theory of the evolution of species. All problems of evolutionary theory are now reduced to the problems of quantum mechanics. However, since we know that these problems are unresolvable in current paradigms of physics (over a century of effort has failed to produce a solution), therefore, there is simply no hope for a theory of evolution unless physics is revised drastically and based on alternative ideas of space, time, causation, and change.

Evolutionary Theory is Pseudoscience

The hypocrisy in biology is overlooking all these issues: (a) insist that change is continuous when we know that continuous change is indeterministic, (b) blame discontinuity on missing fossil records which can never be overcome because every discontinuity will beg even more fossil records, (c) claim that there is a common ancestor when there are hundreds of other visible changes—e.g., in dresses and books—that are successive and yet not evolutionary, and (d) not see the equivalence between the theories of change in biology and in physics, disregarding the deep issues in fundamental physics that hinder any resolution of the problems in evolutionary biology.

This hypocrisy makes the evolutionary theory a pseudoscience because there is no predictive and explanatory power to account for continuous or discrete changes. Moreover, this pseudoscientific idea is also dogmatic because there is no willingness to look at non-evolutionary models of progressive and yet discrete changes (e.g., in fashion or in books) that stare us in the face everywhere.

Evolutionary theory is not a scientific theory, but a dogma in which the materialist *hopes* to explain life-forms based on physical particles and forces. We can fault the dogma, but I'm not going to do that. I will rather send the evolutionist to the physics department, to figure out the problems of indeterminism and discontinuous changes in physics! Don't blame me for doing that, because you—the evolutionist—opened the can of worms by saying that life is nothing more than particles and forces, governed by mathematical laws in space and time. Now that you have asserted those claims so vehemently, please figure out the underlying problems of physics before you say another word.

If you cannot do that, then you have acknowledged yourself to be pseudoscience because all the definitional traits of pseudoscience apply to you: You have a theory that (a) makes no predictions or provides no explanations, (b) it is neither necessary nor sufficient, (c) the causal mechanisms it relies on are deeply flawed, and (d) commonsensical observations about non-evolutionary models of change are disregarded. If instead evolutionary theory is a scientific theory, then everything else that makes no prediction or explanation, that is not necessary or sufficient, that is flawed in its causal models of change, and is contrary to commonsense change, must also be a scientific theory.

Note the irony. I'm not using extraneous standards to judge evolutionary theory. I'm using precisely those standards that evolutionists brag about, applying them back to evolutionists to show that they are not following any of the standards that they brag about.

Any honest self-reflective application of principles of science will reveal that evolutionary theory is not science. It is a lot of data collection, followed by a lot of unsubstantiated claims which contradict the facts, but those contradictions are attributed to missing facts. That doesn't mean that facts don't suggest a change in a succession of species over time; it does. But it also doesn't mean that one species is evolving into another. Evolution is real, but evolutionary theory is not. The evolutionary records are facts; however, the evolutionary theory is not true.

Alternatives to Current Evolution

We can say that evolution is occurring, but the current evolutionary theory does not explain that evolution. More precisely, the facts of fossil records do not imply the *evolution of species*—i.e., one species evolving into another, which is also called *descent with modification*. The facts only tell us that species appear one after another, quite like new books appear successively although they are not produced from previous books through copy and modification. Likewise, new dresses are not produced from previous dresses by copy and modification.

How that happens, is a separate topic, which I will not get into this post. But if you are interested, then the book Signs of Life discusses the above issues, apart from other arguments against evolutionary theory (drawn from computational theory, game theory, and complex system dynamics), and presents a non-evolutionary theory of evolution in which species appear like successive dresses or books. Like the problems I outlined above, this alternative model of evolution requires a change in the theoretical landscape in terms of the understanding of space, time, causation, and change, to recover necessity and sufficiency, predictive and explanatory completeness, and destroy mathematical indeterminism. But as you can tell, this is also a need for physics, because biology is not a unique science anyway.

How Quantity Science Emerged from Quality Science

Numbers: Truth vs. Usefulness

Even as I often criticize quantity thinking, I don't mean to say that it is completely useless. Many quantitative truths are pervasively true. $2 + 2 = 4$ in all situations, for example. This truth can be used for practical purposes like counting the number of people, animals, and houses. Numbers can be used for financial accounting. We can use a flat-space geometry for astronomical calculations of time because we can discount the effects of planets on our bodies and minds. Flat-space geometry can be used for many things in city planning. We can use algebra and converging infinite series to compute the lengths of arcs and lines.

Thus, one is led to the question: How can something so useful be false? This article discusses the answer, along with how this usefulness may have been transformed into the truth and reality. The conclusion is: All that is true is also useful, but all that is useful is not true.

The Problem of Counting Things

The problem with quantity thinking is that there is no logical foundation for numbers. Every attempt to give numbers a foundation has either relied on numbers (e.g., that 0 depends on 1 or 2), or it has ended up in logical contradictions (e.g., those based on set theory). That is because quantities, numbers, and counting rest upon the foundation of qualities.

Whenever we count two things, animals, or people, they are always distinct as qualities. For instance, we have to identify things as red, green, and blue, then by seeing that red is not green or blue, we distinguish them as separate entities, and then by prioritizing red over green over blue, we can sequence them into first, second, and third. Quantities are the *effect* of qualities but that effect can ignore the qualities based on which we distinguished them.

For instance, while counting people, we ignore their nationalities, colors, languages, cultures, genders, etc. and each person is counted as one person, regardless of the fact that some person is more or less capable, a socially superior or inferior person, a good or bad person. This equality is an illusion created by disregarding their qualitative differences. The fact is that if these qualities did not exist, then counting would also not exist. Hence, numbers are not a fundamental reality because they are always based on the effect of quality differences.

Practical Usefulness of Numbers

And yet, there are situations in which we do not need to know the quality differences. A merchant, for instance, can value all his goods in a single currency, and add up the total value. This summing of total value disregards the fact that each individual thing has a value based on its qualities. If we were using a barter system of goods exchange, then we would rely on the qualities of things being exchanged. If, however, we use the currency to denominate the value of things, then we can add up the total value and ignore the quality differences. That neglect is sometimes convenient but it cannot be the foundation on which we always study reality.

Quantitative sciences were formulated in India for cases where such neglect was convenient. The Roman numeral system is useless if we use it to balance an account that involves expenses and liabilities because it requires negative numbers, which then require a zero. The number associated with income, asset, expense, or liability is based on a quality, but in a balance sheet with disparate quality things, it is convenient to convert them into a quantity. Similarly, algebra and geometry were formulated in India for temple and city construction and time calculation. However, these quantitative sciences were restricted to certain limited use cases, and they were never considered to be on par with the Vedic texts, nor even a true description of nature.

The Spread of Quantity Science

Due to trade relations between India and other countries, the system of accounting spread to other parts of the world. Likewise, when foreigners came to India, they saw city planning, temples, and architectures, and they began to see the usefulness of numbers, algebra, and geometry. Then, many masons traveled to other parts of the world to consult and construct temples and cities and passed on their knowledge of algebra and geometry to others.

Historically, geometry and algebra were associated in Europe with masons. They employed a combination of qualities and quantities. In India, this practical use of geometry and algebra is called Vāstu-Shastra or the "scripture on things". In modern time, this is called 'architecture'. The difference is that Vāstu-Shastra associates directions, shapes, and sizes with meanings.

The direction, shape, and size itself is geometry and algebra, but the meaning tied to it is based on qualities. This quality science pervaded masonry in the use of astrology and astronomy for architecture. For instance, the shadows cast by the planetary movement were given significance in the construction of temples and cities. The significance comes from astrology and the movement from astronomical calculations. Masons were thus well-versed in mathematics and astronomy, and they employed a science of both quantities and qualities to create architectures.

Vāstu-Shastra, which employs such a combination of qualities and quantities came to be known as *masonry* in other parts of the world. When Christianity arose in Europe, the masons were persecuted like pagans, because they were using astrological principles and a science of qualities, while Christians considered these things paganism. That led to the formation of secret societies, and distrust between masonry and Christianity was common. Even today, some people associate these secret masonic societies with something evil, because they have been considered evil since the time of Roman Catholicism. However, the masons were still building exquisite Cathedrals all over Europe, and their knowledge—although declining—was kept alive in some form.

The Development of Modern Science

A transformation occurred in the 17th century due to the Protestant Reformation: (a) Cathedral construction declined because Protestants rejected Catholicism, leading to a decline in masonic membership, (b) it gave masons freedom from Catholic persecution, (c) Protestants became interested in masonry ideas, and (d) masonry started accepting outsiders, adding ideas from other cults. This transformation converted masonry into the modern freemasonry movement.

The Royal Society of England in the 17th century had many freemasons, including Isaac Newton. It is sometimes speculated (see the book Isaac Newton and Freemasonry by Alain Bauer) that Newton borrowed many masonic ideas to create his mechanics. But it is hard to be sure because he burned all the original papers, and none of the original drafts of Principia—which should detail how he worked out his mechanics to its final form—are to be found. After his death, Newton's heir hid most of his writing to obfuscate the origins of his work. Most of Newton's writing was not publicly available until the 1960s, and after that, researchers have dismissed connections between his calculus, physics, and freemasonry. It is hard to believe that. You cannot regard Newton as a genius on one hand, and a split-brain thinker on the other. Even if everything is not consistent, there are bound to be significant connections.

More accurate evidence comes from the historical precedents of infinite series expansions of functions such as sine and cosine, and numbers such as pi, in Indian mathematics, that precede the development of calculus by 300 years. Calculus inverts these expansions into summations. It is quite possible, although not certainly known today, that Newton got these via masonry sources but burned the original papers, and his heirs covered up his tracks for a very long time.

The fact that these calculations existed in India, does not mean that they denoted planetary movement. The Vedic understanding of planetary movement is that the locations and directions in space are represented by different qualities and the planets go around due to cyclical change in qualities as an effect of cyclical time. The time we measure as a result of planetary motion is an *effect* of Causal Time. Likewise, the trajectories drawn on paper are just a picture useful for temple construction, never to be confused with the cosmos. Newton applied such architecture models back to the cosmos by postulating that space is uniform and time is linear, attributing the motion to a gravitational force. He was most likely aided by the work that Indian mathematicians had done for architecture, although he misused it to describe the nature of the cosmos.

Masonry is an important bridge between quality and quantity thinking because masons need mathematical models to estimate the effects of planetary movement on the temple. But if that model is treated as that of planetary movement, then we are stepping outside the bounds of what the model was supposed to achieve. When Newton imputed these masonry models back to the cosmos, he stripped masonry of the science of qualities and gave birth to modern science.

Antecedents to Modern Masonry

In a sense, it is true that modern science emerged out of numbers, algebra, and geometry that the masons had originally developed in India. However, it is also true that what the West took out of this masonry was the science of quantities, and left out the system of qualities. Masonry was the perfect recipe for this because it was using a combination of quantities and qualities. Thereby, something developed in India became completely antithetical to the original Vedic ideas.

Masonry, however, is not an ancient science. Even until 5000 years ago, the most important cities were built either by demigods or through mystic power. The Mahabharata notes that cities like Indraprastha and Dwaraka were built by the demigod Vishwakarma. Even Lanka was built by Vishwakarma and rebuilt in a day when it was burnt by Hanuman. Similarly, temples were not formerly constructed in India, because practically everyone worshipped the deity at home.

Historians estimate that temple construction in India began

during the Gupta period around the 3rd century CE, which is also considered the golden age of mathematicians like Aryabhatta and Baskaracharya who created Indian astronomy and mathematics. It is not therefore farfetched to assert that astronomy and mathematics were created in India mainly for temple construction.

Masonry is therefore exclusively a Kali-yuga "science", and it was born in India in the last few thousand years due to the need for constructing cities and temples. Great kings wanted to show their power and wealth by constructing big cities and temples, and that gave birth to masonry. Through trade with other countries, this knowledge spread to other places too. However, after the successive foreign invasions, the destruction of temples, the reduction in the building of new forts, cities, and temples based on masonry principles, and the hands of masons being cut-off after they had created great architectures, masonry died in India. Modern temple constructions, for instance, use professional architects who know almost nothing about the effects of architecture on the body and mind, the role of planetary movement, and how to use it effectively.

In contrast, during Greek times, Plato associated meanings with various shapes. The tetrahedron was fire, the cube was earth, the octahedron was air, and the icosahedron was water. Egyptians entombed their Pharaohs in pyramids because they were sun-worshippers, and their Pharaoh was a descendant of the sun-god on earth, the sun was fire, and the fire was symbolized in a tetrahedron. By entombing the Pharaoh in a Pyramid, his body was effectively encased inside the sun.

Quality vs. Quantity Sciences in India

When people talk about advanced sciences in ancient India, they almost always refer to masonry, because it is the thing that most people associate with numbers, algebra, and geometry. You can talk about the advanced architecture of temples, and how they were tied to planetary movement. We can do astronomy based on these quantity sciences, however, we cannot do astrology, because astrology requires associating directions, objects, and forms with meanings.

Practically everyone has forgotten the much older science of qualities, based on non-binary logic, to the point where even the mention of the fact that binary logic is false, that numerical sciences can never be the real descriptions of nature, etc. raises eyebrows everywhere. This is because people everywhere have accepted that masonry is the basis of all knowledge.

Brahmana vs. Sudra Sciences

In the Vedic system, masonry will be called a *Sudra science,* because a mason is a *Sudra*. Of course, Sudras can be very intelligent; they can do advanced astronomy, mathematics, architecture. But they are called Sudra because they work with inanimate things. They were influenced by the other classes in the sense that they associated qualities with places, things, and directions. However, because this knowledge applies to inanimate things, their knowledge is the lowest. Qualities were more prominent for Vaishyas as they worked with animals and plants. They were even more prominent for Kshatriyas who organized human society. And they were most prominent for Brahmanas who were thinking and speaking about the superhumans.

Modern science is based on the lowest technical knowledge of masonry after it had been stripped of qualities. In a sense, it is less than Sudra knowledge, but it wants to define the superhuman.

If we understand the origins of quantity science, how it arose when the contact with demigods ceased, how it has practical usefulness—sometimes when not totally stripped of qualities, and at other times in a limited sense when totally stripped of qualities—and yet, it is not the basis on which to model reality, then we can distinguish between two kinds of science based on qualities and quantity. The quantity science, when not totally stripped of qualities, is a *Sudra* science, and has practical usefulness in building cities, buildings, houses, and other things. Then, the science completely focused on qualities, the understanding of life, the universe, soul, and God, is *Brahmana* science. These two can co-exist if we know which one is better and why.

While doing architecture, the science of qualities decides the relative locations, shapes, heights, and elevations of different structures, but once those things have been decided, other things can be done based on quantities. Architecture is not just about aesthetics, or what looks good to the eye. It is about invoking cosmic and human principles to design a structure in harmony with the cosmos, and suited to humans. The building is ādibhautika, but it has to be compatible with the ādiātmika (the human body and mind), and the ādidaivika (the cosmic structure). That requires us to understand how the cosmos influences ordinary buildings, and how those buildings then affect the human inhabitants. When we view architecture in this broader sense, ranging from the cosmos to the human mind, then we can understand how masons were required to be mathematically, astronomically, and astrologically astute, and yet, they were still Sudras.

This quantity science has limited applicability to inanimate things, while the quality science lies at the foundation of even how inanimate things are counted. The quantity science uses many simplifying assumptions—e.g., all things are qualitatively identical, space is uniform, time is linear, things being modeled have no mind, that each thing is indeed separate from other things—which are true to limited extents for inanimate objects, but not true in general. If we limit the simplifying assumptions to some cases, then quantity sciences can be pragmatically useful, although not true. The truth is always useful, but the useful is not always true.

Non-Dualism, Inseparability, and Entanglement

Revolutionary vs. Incremental History

In an article called Laws of Increasing and Decreasing Returns, I made a pithy remark in passing—Progressive history doesn't have revolutions and paradigm changes. I will use this article to explain how this is a consequence of the modern scientific assumptions about the *separation* of locations, times, and things. Separation allows us to count things, and describe them using mathematical equations. But it takes away the ability to explain phenomena resulting from the *entanglement* of things.

Revolutions in history are the result of such entanglements between past, present, and future. That doesn't happen always. Hence, revolutions are rare. But they are also inexplicable in a worldview of separation, which mandates that changes must be linear and incremental, never disruptive, drastic, or revolutionary. Thereby, we can never construct a scientific theory of history, if by science we mean separation of things and it involves revolutions. There are literally infinite inexplicable phenomena outside the reach of current science because they necessitate entanglement which modern science rejects. The situations in which separation can be applied to a reasonable degree of approximation are very small. Thereby, we can reap high returns on investment in the early stages—when science is used to model those phenomena where separability is valid to a reasonable degree of approximation. But as science progresses, it runs out of such things to model. Instead, it runs into things that are not truly separable. This is the phase of diminishing and negative returns in science.

I will begin with the natural science consequences of separation and then discuss the cultural context and history of these ideas toward the end. Due to the presence of the same cultural context in all subjects, the problem is not limited to one or two subjects. It is present in every modern subject. If you haven't read that article, I will suggest reading it now.

Brief Summary of the Previous Article

Thomas Kuhn assumed that cyclical history can be progressive, but that is not necessary—cycles can also be regressive and/or repetitive. These cycles become progressive or regressive based on a criterion that I described as non-duality vs. duality.

However, an illusion of progress can sometimes be created as we shift from one kind of dualism to another. For example, if the duality of bourgeoisie vs. proletariat is replaced by the duality of freedom vs. regulation, then, for a while, we see a discrete change called a revolution. But after some time, the regulators become bourgeoisie (and vice versa) and the regulated become the proletariat (and vice versa), because the duality wasn't solved by replacing one dualism with another. The solution to the original dualism is unifying society by everyone performing their duty with the common purpose of uplifting society as a whole. If instead, we give each person equal rights to uplift themselves through competition with others, then there will be many more tyrants than before. It is easier to revolt against a common tyrant, and harder to revolt against many tyrants. This normalizes tyranny more than before.

The substitution of one duality by another (through a revolution) creates a short jump within a cycle of diminishing returns. By the time the new cycle completes, the situation can be worse than before. Therefore, historical revolutions that merely substitute dualisms cannot be considered progress.

Kuhn was motivated by socio-political revolutions in history—Russian, French, and American revolutions. He imagined that such revolutions can also occur in science. But he was also cynical about these revolutions leading to perfect outcomes; future revolutions were imminent in his view. But Kuhn assumed that these revolutions were progressive when they can also be regressive.

Ideas of progressive time have been lingering in Western thinking for over two millennia. Under this view, the present is necessarily better than the past, and the future will be even better. It is a lazy solution to the problem of motivating people into action—don't worry, the future is bright! We should examine it.

Kuhn realized that progress cannot occur routinely if we are stuck in the rut of repeating past mistakes. It must happen due to occasional revolutions. However, revolutions (discontinuous and non-smooth changes) are contrary to the basic paradigm of modern science. Due to this, discontinuous and non-smooth changes cannot occur within current scientific assumptions.

The Need for Continuity in Calculus

Anyone who has studied high-school calculus knows that calculus mandates *smooth and continuous curves*. Continuity means that a curve cannot have breaks. Smoothness means there cannot be sudden shifts in the direction of motion. A saw-toothed wave or a square wave are easy counterexamples.

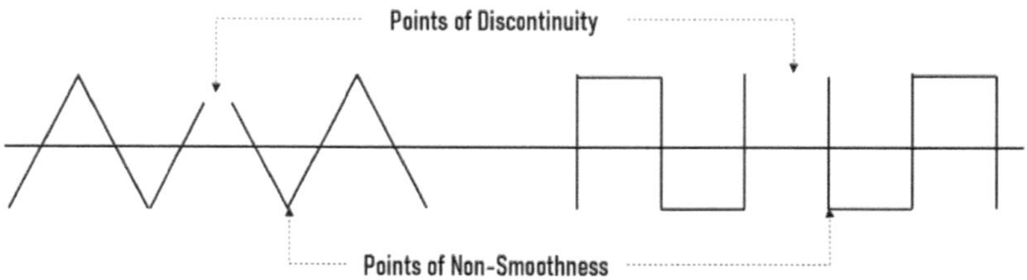

At the occurrences of discontinuity in any line or surface, dx/dy is *undefined*. And at the occurrences of non-smoothness, dx/dy is *infinite*. If we permit these in calculus, then all current causal and explanatory models collapse.

At the occurrences of discontinuity, a particle must go from A to B without going through anything in between. That can happen if the space between A and B doesn't exist. At the point of non-smoothness, something is moving in one direction at A and in another direction at B, and there is nothing in between them. That can happen only if the time between A and B ceases to exist.

If we don't postulate space and time disappearing and appearing, then we can postulate that matter or force appears and disappears. At the discontinuity, matter disappears at A and appears at B. Likewise, at the occurrence of non-smoothness, infinite force appears for a moment and then disappears after that to change the direction of motion of an object. All these infinities violate conservation laws (although for the briefest durations and distances).

The Problem of Historical Revolutions

To explain historical revolutions, we have to contend with the same problems that forced us to abandon discontinuity and non-smoothness in calculus. After all, a revolution is either a discontinuous change (i.e., that we are A and then we are B without going through anything in between) or a non-smooth change (i.e., that we were moving in direction A and then in direction B due to an infinite force for a moment in time). If our notions of space, time, or causality break down in calculus as a result of discontinuous and non-smooth changes in mechanics, then how can we explain or predict their occurrence in history?

If the cause of revolution always exists, then why doesn't it always act? What causes long periods of stability or incremental change? If instead, the cause of revolution doesn't exist for long periods, then how can it suddenly appear? Since revolutions have occurred and can occur, therefore, the assumptions of continuity and smoothness in calculus cannot explain their occurrence. Likewise, we have to discard the assumptions underlying calculus and reimagine causality, to explain discontinuous and unsmooth changes.

What Historical Revolutions Require

Discontinuities in history occur due to the *memory* of the past. A discontinuous change doesn't happen at the first instance of a problem. Rather, we try to solve that problem using existing methods, within the pre-established framework (perhaps established by a previous revolution). It is only when many such attempts have been made and found to fail, that a discontinuous change occurs. Now imagine for the moment that we did not remember the past, including the failed attempts to solve a problem. Every new attempt would be the *first* such attempt, and it would never lead to a revolutionary change.

A discontinuous change occurs because history *accumulates* in our memory, and reaches a tipping point. A massive force of change appears suddenly because the memory of failures overwhelms the current idea of reality. This is not a violation of conservation laws in the classical sense of energy conservation because the past existed in the present before it caused a revolution. This is a violation of the idea that the future is entirely determined by the *observable* present. History is not an observable present. It lies dormant and is activated occasionally. To explain disruptive revolutions, we have to postulate a new kind of existence—memory—as the past existing and acting in the present.

Likewise, discontinuities in history occur due to a different vision of the future. We can predict the future state if we stay on the same trajectory, and we may not want that state. We change the vision of the future, and that in turn leads to a revolution, which then alters the future. If we did not have a vision of the future, or if we did not mind the future state given by the present trajectory, then there would be no discontinuity in the trajectory. The future will be just the next state of the present state, and each successive state would be determined by the *previous* rather than the *future* state.

Alternative visions of the future, however, do not automatically lead to a revolution. Rather, we try to attain the said vision within the pre-established framework. It is only when many of those attempts have failed, and the memory of the previous failures reaches a tipping point, that the revolution is triggered.

Hence, a revolution will not occur if we don't have a vision of the future—if we don't know where we want to go, there is no need to change the current trajectory. And it will not occur if we don't have a memory of the past—we don't want to break what is working at the first instance of a problem.

Discontinuous and unsmooth changes occur if and only if the past and the future exist in the present as an *idea*. That idea must interact with the world, and produce a discontinuity and/or non-smoothness. The postulates of continuity and smoothness in calculus are thus conceptually equivalent to two other formulations: (a) there are no ideas interacting with matter in the present, and (b) the past and the future do not exist in the present. By eliminating ideas from our scientific vocabulary, we also remove the past and the future from scientific causality, because these exist in the present as ideas. By these two kinds of removals from the model of causation, we construct calculus in which discontinuities and non-smooth changes are forbidden.

Science Makes Revolutions Impossible

When the mind is removed from science, then ideas lose causal efficacy. These include ideas about the past, the present, and the future. The past is called memory, the present is called knowledge, and the future is called a goal. An idea can *refer to* and *represent* something other than itself. It is a symbol of some reality. The physical idea of nature replaces symbols with things in themselves. Once we remove ideas, then we remove goals, memories, and knowledge. The result is not just the negation of the mind. It is also the inability to predict or explain discontinuous and unsmooth changes. Now, history can only be *smooth and continuous curves*. Revolutions in history are impossible.

When Thomas Kuhn employed the notion of revolutions in scientific models, he was bringing the idea of disruptive changes from American, French, and Russian revolutions into science to construct a historical trajectory in which long-term stability was occasionally punctuated by disruptive changes. However, he assumed that humans have *ideas*—memories, goals, and knowledge—which are valid assumptions in cultural, social, political, and economic revolutions but untenable hypotheses in current science.

Kuhn's extensions of cultural-social-political-economic revolutions into those of scientific models contradict the foundational assumptions of science since Newton's time. We can either have revolutions and reject calculus, or keep calculus and reject revolutions. The problem of reconciling historical revolutions (caused by knowledge, goals, and memories) with the fundamental assumptions of science involves an irreconcilable *dualism*.

For mechanical problems, we can use calculus and reject ideas. For human problems, we can use ideas and reject calculus. But for understanding the historical evolution of science, we need both. In fact, the scientific revolution can now be predicated upon a *model crisis*—that many observable facts do not fit the current scientific paradigm without breaking it in fundamental ways.

The paradigm shift must now entail (a) the existence of ideas, (b) the existence of the past and the future as ideas, and (c) the interaction of those ideas with the world, causing different outcomes. Science must study such interactions.

The knowledge of the world interacts with the present state of the world to create what Kuhn would call "normal science"—i.e., solving problems within pre-established frameworks. The knowledge of the world interacts with a changing world to create what Kuhn would call "model drift"—i.e., incremental tweaking of existing models. But the interaction of the memories of the past and the goals about the future cause what Kuhn would call "model crisis", "model revolution", and "paradigm shift". We are able to conveniently ignore the role of ideas in science if things seem to move continuously and smoothly. We cannot ignore those roles in the case of discontinuous and non-smooth changes.

Solving the Mind-Body Problem

The answer to the mind-body problem—essential to explaining how the future and the past interact with the present—is treating the body also as an idea. That idea is not *private*. It is also public. The mistake of Cartesian dualism is to make ideas *private*. They are not private. Our memories and goals are separate from the conscious observer because we are not always conscious of them. Descartes collapsed the distinction between thought and consciousness when he said—I think therefore I exist. He equated the self with thought, making all thought private. He dissociated this self and thought from the body, and made matter public. Thus, ideas are private and matter is public. Science is about the public stuff, and religion is about the private stuff. Ideas must be excluded from science because they are private. Science must be restricted to the public stuff.

Once thoughts are private, they cannot interact with something public—i.e., matter—creating the mind-body dualism, because wherever the interaction occurs, the mind becomes the body or the body becomes the mind. So, a science of material substance is formulated keeping the thinking substance out of science. Within the material substance, the past and the future cannot causally influence the present, making many phenomena inexplicable.

The entire succession of ideas that begins by equating the self with thought is false. However, it produces useful results in the beginning, becomes useless after some time, and eventually becomes harmful. This is the progression within a mind-body dualism that leads to diminishing and negative outcomes.

If both mind and body are ideas, then there is no mind-body problem, because mind-body interaction is the interaction between two sets of ideas. They are just different kinds of ideas—some more abstract than others. The ideas are not private, and not inside consciousness. They are public realities. In that public reality, past, present, and future exist in the present as ideas—memory, knowledge, and goal. Causality pertains to their interactions.

Once we remove the mind-body problem, then there is a different problem of how consciousness interacts with ideas which I will not discuss here because: (a) it changes our focus, and (b) it is not relevant to the problem of revolutions, discontinuous, non-smooth changes, past, present, and future interactions. The mind-body problem is a fictional construct and the cause of numerous other issues. If we drop that by suitable revisions to reality, then all those dualisms disappear at once. The problem of consciousness is whether we are presently *aware* of our memory, knowledge, and goals. These are not the same issue.

Summarizing the Problem and the Solution

This long discussion was necessary to explain the statement: Progressive history doesn't have revolutions and paradigm changes. This is because (1) progressive history is also continuous and smooth trajectories, (2) such trajectories are based on the current state, rather than the past or future states, and (3) without a causal role for the past and the future, there can be no discontinuous or discrete changes, i.e., revolutions and paradigm changes.

When Kuhn talks about revolutionary progress through cycles, he employs ideas from socio-cultural-political revolutions, which permit the existence of memories and goals causally influencing the present. Those assumptions are incompatible with modern science. By using ideas incompatible with science to depict the progress of science, a double standard about the mind is created in science. The mind exists to permit knowledge, memory, and goals, and to aid in the progress of science—including revolutions in science. However, the mind doesn't exist in the causal scientific picture of causality. There, we will use calculus, eliminate the role of past and future, and the influence of the mind on the present reality. These double standards are a typical part of mainstream scientific rhetoric. They mislead the innocent. But they also result in a system of diminishing and negative returns unless we change our rhetoric.

When history involves revolutions and paradigm changes, then it is also helical, and hence history rhymes with itself. Thereby we can assert two things— (1) progressive history under modern materialism is devoid of revolutions, and (2) revolutions that lead to progress are also helical due to idea-like reality.

The cause of disruptive change is memories and goals. We try to solve problems within the current paradigm, but if the attempted solutions fail, we remember those failures. As that memory of failure accumulates, at some point it contradicts our goals more than before. That triggers a revolution. This change is helical—it is cyclical but it can be progressive or regressive.

Envisioning an Alternative Science

This solution to the general problem of history is incomplete without translating it into a scientific paradigm. That is what I will turn toward now. It involves reconceiving quantum entanglement. Under this conception, there are three fundamental kinds of ideas—memories of the past, goals about the future, and consequences of history. The memories of the past limit what we can imagine or conceive at present. The goals about the future limit what we want to imagine or conceive in the future. And consequences of history limit the interactions with the world which will limit the attainment of the goals at present. We can call these *could, would,* and *should*. We can also call these the conceptual representations of past, future, and present—if we understand that they are an individual's ideas about the past, future, and present.

These three kinds of ideas are also potentialities—i.e., they are not always active—and structured hierarchically because ideas must always be structured from abstract to contingent. We can also say that these hierarchies constitute three kinds of spaces. They lie dormant and inactive as potentials.

Change pertains to the *mixing* of these three kinds of ideas—every change is the mixture of some parts of three kinds of space to construct a *perceived space* that has no fundamental reality (because it is constructed from an unperceived reality). That mixing is caused by time. The perceived space can be called an appearance and the underlying space and time can be called reality.

Whatever we call quantum entanglement pertains to (1) the hierarchical structure of ideas in which ideas are mutually entangled, (2) the mixing of these three kinds of ideas by time to create an experience, and (3) the effect of experience back on the sources that were mixed to alter our memories, goals, and consequences. These must be considered entangled because (1) hierarchies necessitate similarities, (2) their mixing requires compatibility, and (3) the same experience doesn't have the same effects on everyone; the effect depends on their present goals, memories, and consequences.

Implications of the Alternative Science

The result of this model is that whatever we call a planet is also a person, and planetary phenomena are also the result of the mixing of their memories, goals, and consequences. We are parts of the planet in the sense that our memories, goals, and consequences are the subsets of the planetary memories, goals, and consequences. Likewise, whatever we call a universe is also a person, comprising the planets. Planetary and cosmic phenomena are hence the experiences of different kinds of persons. Some experiences are more detailed or "microscopic" while others are more abstract or "macroscopic".

The perception of a table at present depends on (a) whether we have access to a table, (b) whether we know what a table is, and (c) whether we want to see it as a table. If we don't have access to a table, then we will not perceive it. If we don't know what a table is from the past, then we cannot construct knowledge of the table in the present; we will perceive it as a curious structure of wood parts. If we don't want something to be a table, then despite the fact that it could be a table based on past memories, it will be something other than a table, although based on what we want it to be. Therefore, experience has three causes.

The present picture of reality—or what we call experience—itself depends on the access to some reality and its classification into categories and concepts based on our memories and goals. Observation cannot be described without invoking a causal role for past and future ideas onto the present observable. And observation cannot be described without the observer having access to the reality being observed. Experience depends on memory, goal, and reality.

This is the *personalization* of nature. The Earth has a duty to give resources. And we have a duty to use those resources frugally. We can take the minimum required, and be grateful for what we get. This is because Earth is a person. Just as society is bound together by duties, likewise, Earth and humans are bound by the mutual performance of duties toward each other. If those duties are disregarded, then there will be punishment. Likewise, if the Earth is exploited, there will be punishment—people will be deprived of resources. The relationship between Earth and humans is based on the mutual performance of duties, in contrast to the idea that man has dominion over nature.

Through such personalization of nature and duties, we can describe a planet and the universe in the same way that we describe our experiences. There is no dualism of man vs. nature. And we describe our experiences not just based on external objective reality but also based on concepts and categories acquired in our past and present. The interaction between concepts and reality creates no problem because that reality is also an idea. It is not a material substance. It is rather the memories, goals, and consequences of some person.

Solving the Entanglement Problem

Quantum theory presents issues of entanglement because we are accustomed to the classical mechanical separation of objects. The past, present, and future must be separable; a change to the future cannot change the past, although the immediate past can determine the present. Components of an ensemble must be strictly separable particles; they cannot be mutually entangled to form an irreducible whole. If separability is false, then everything else fails.

Separation also means that the observer sees the world from outside the world. The observed can affect the observer, but not vice versa; if the observer affects the observed, then it would not be objective knowledge. It would be an observer's viewpoint interfering with reality. If the observer grouped things into ensembles of his choosing, then that grouping has no implications on reality, because that grouping only exists in the observer's mind.

If we drop separability, then particles in an ensemble are structured into a whole via a hierarchy. Two interacting things are not separable—they select parts for interaction such that multiple perspective measurements are needed to fully understand anything. The past, present, and future are not separable because what we experience at present is influenced by the memories acquired in the past and goals pertaining to the future. Hierarchies in the larger ensembles entangle some things but not the other things. Some time in the past has a greater influence on the present and the future as compared to other times. By changing our goals about the future, we can alter the memory of the past, and vice versa, because goals are entangled with our memory of our past. Changes to goals and memories are not factual changes to the future and past, and yet, those changes have an effect in the present and can alter the future.

When winners write history, they select and modify facts to suit their victorious agenda. That history exists in the present, but it need not be factual. Changes to historical records are not factual changes to the past. They are changes to our memory of the past. By reading altered histories, people create goals of grandeur in the future. Those goals are not the factual future. They are realities that exist in the present and they can change the future. However, those goals may not be realized exactly in the future. However, memory and goal become past and future, when we refuse to include ideas in science.

Problems Rooted in Physical Conceptions

Entanglement is a problem in physics if we equate the *idea* of the past and the future to the past and the future. This happens in a physical conception of reality. Entanglement is a problem in physics if interactions between two particles are unique to a pair of particles, and the principles of interaction cannot be universalized. Universalization happens in a physical conception of reality. Entanglement is a problem in physics if things at one location have far greater effects on some locations vs. others as a result of hierarchies. Uniformity of locations and their effects is the cornerstone of all physical laws.

The problem in current scientific thinking is that the past and the future cannot entangle without violating the conditions of separability. Hence, time quantization creates problems. Two things in different locations cannot entangle without violating the conditions of separability. Hence, matter quantization creates problems. One location cannot have greater or lesser effects on other locations without breaking separability. Hence space quantization creates problems. All classical physical assumptions about separability create problems. Since these assumptions utilize calculus, which depends on the uniformity of space, time, and matter, therefore, trying to fit reality into equations of calculus is also equally problematic.

Since scientists are attached to physical conceptions, separability, numbers, and calculus, a change is unlikely. They have walked down a path for more than three centuries. They cannot reject it, even if it entails diminishing and negative returns. This is a problem of preconceived ideas, attachment to those ideas, and reluctance to change them. Any meaningful change requires us to go back to the drawing slate and discuss problematic ideas like mind-body dualism and notions of knowledge that separate the knower from the known.

Alternative Sources of Intuition

All scientific knowledge is the generalization of some human experience. However, there is infinite freedom in picking which human experiences to generalize from. Modern science chose billiard balls and vibrating strings to generalize from. But we can also pick a different experience.

If we keep our life compartmentalized into many separate domains, such that work and home are separate disentangled realities, then problems at work don't create problems at home. But since work and home can be entangled into a single ensemble, hence, work can impact home and vice versa. Since work and home can be disentangled, therefore, separability is a subset of entanglement. There is no need to reduce an entangled reality to a separable reality. It is sufficient to say that at some times, some places, some things are not entangled with other things at other times and other places. And yet, you will see physicists hell-bent on trying to reduce an entangled reality to a separable reality. Why? It is because they *want* to see the world as separable things. They don't want entangled things. A predetermined agenda drives their research.

They also want to separate the observer from the observed, never mind how false it is. For example, if we meet a person and we don't know that they hold a prestigious position in society, we treat them like ordinary people. But if we know about their social status, then we treat them with respect. So, how can we say that the observer's knowledge of reality has no effect on the observed outcomes? Isn't the demonstration of respect based on our knowledge of their social status? Similarly, it is well known that people hear concert musicians when they perform in a concert hall, but ignore them when they perform in the railway station. Doesn't this mean that our knowledge of reality changes reality? But you will see scientists hell-bent on separating reality from our knowledge of reality. Reality can change knowledge, but knowledge cannot change reality. That is because they want to keep ideas and minds out of science.

All problems of modern science are rooted in trying to universalize billiard balls and vibrating strings as the cardinal examples of causality while designating the far more common lived experience as epiphenomena of billiard balls and vibrating strings. That is a *choice* that Western thinking made. It is not the only choice. We can reverse that choice by making lived experience the cardinal examples of causality and then explain vibrating strings and billiard balls based on it. One is not more fundamental than another *a priori*. One is not simpler than the other *a priori*. One is not better than the other *a priori*. Those have to be judged by how much unity they bring in our knowledge.

If we begin with the idea of separation while reality is inseparable, then we will be compelled to create thousands of models to capture inseparability through a different model of separability. None of those models will ever be perfect. The problems with those models will compel us to increase the number of models, and the process leads to diminishing and negative returns.

Ideological Roots of Modern Science

Why are billiard balls sources of intuition about reality? The answer is that separability applies to them to a fairly reasonable level of approximation. Why are vibrating strings sources of intuition about reality? It is because we can reduce a vibrating string to a set of connected particles—pushing and pulling each other—rather easily, and we already want to view the world in terms of separable things even if that is only an approximation. Reducing the whole to its parts, treating them as independent entities, and describing changes to them using push and pull forces is the foundation of modern science.

But it is harder to grasp these ideas in modern science without the larger context of Western civilization. Western civilization is a story of increasing individualism. It reached a tipping point during the Renaissance when the focus of art on the divine was rejected, and artists could choose whatever mundane subjects they desired to depict; portraits of people and landscapes of nature became possible due to this change. It reached another tipping point during Reformation in Europe when the special rights of the priests to determine religious beliefs were abolished giving each person the right to choose their religious beliefs. It reached another tipping point during Enlightenment when nature was divided into independent particles in Newton's mechanics. And it reached yet another tipping point during the French Revolution when the special rights of kings were rejected giving equal rights to everyone, bringing the government under ordinary people's control, rather than an authority over them. At each step, individualism grew in strength and popularity.

Historians use grandiloquent names like Renaissance, Reformation, Englightenment, and Revolution to demarcate various phases in this longer trajectory. But they are different stages of growing individualism that span art, religion, nature, and society over time. They are superficially different, but in a deeper sense either quite similar or completely identical. After a few of these, new names for the stages that follow are unnecessary, because each of these trends affirms, solidifies, and emboldens the other trends.

The trajectory toward greater individualism in personal life is closely related to the atomization of matter. We always see the world in the same way we see ourselves. The liar thinks that everyone is a liar. The hard worker thinks that everyone is hardworking. The world is modeled after the same principles as the self. If the self is individualistic and considers itself separate from others, then the world is modeled as separable things. Science now tries to reduce all complexity to simplicity—simplicity being defined as the separation of things. If we cannot separate things from each other, then complexity cannot be simplified. The irreducible unit of reality is the thing in itself.

Everything has to be atomized because that is how the ideology of separation *models* reality. If things are modeled, then they can be controlled. If reality is entangled, then it cannot be modeled and controlled. If a society is collectivist, then its internal interactions cannot be demystified and described. Societal structures like family and community must be broken down into atomized individuals working for their self-interest in order for rational principles to be applied to them. The shared culture or history that binds people must be replaced by individualism to gain control over them. Once they are divided and separated, then they can be aggregated using a "rules-based order". A religion that encourages individualism becomes the handmaiden of atomization.

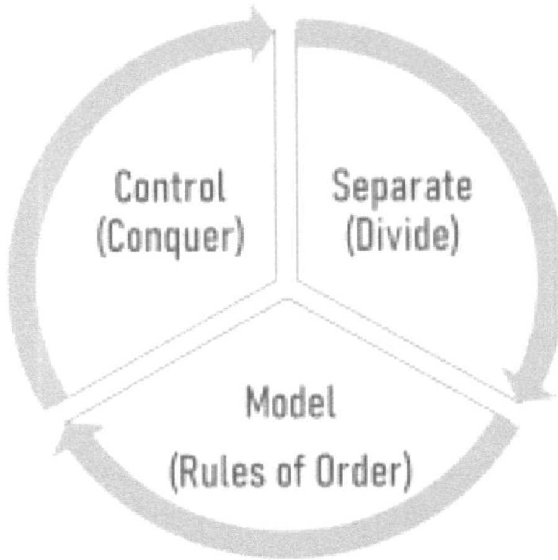

Divide and conquer are two mutually reinforcing sides of a coin. As you divide more, you create more models, control more using those models, and use that control to divide more. Separation leads to scientific models, which then leads to control, which leads to more separation, and so on. The same principles can therefore be repeatedly utilized to divide and rule nations, people, and things.

Obedience to the rules-based order creates outward cleanliness or systematization and everything looks well-organized. But this is temporary because the rule-maker is individualistic. He is not interested in the collective good, as the rulers should be. He is solely interested in his personal good. He keeps changing the rules to gain more wealth and power. When others realize that the rules are meant to benefit the rule-makers rather than everyone, they stop following the rules. The enforcement of rules leads to conflict and destroys order. The situation after the destruction of this rules-based order is worse than what it was before the rules-based order appeared on the scene.

Since the end of the rules-based order is worse than what immediately preceded it, therefore, the end is delayed by elongating the phase of diminishing and negative returns. It is considered the lesser of two evils. People cannot see why this end was predetermined from the start, and how it creates the possibility of a new start, which can be never-ending progress if we solve the prior dualisms that had made the collapse imminent. Instead, they will always say: Look, the destruction of the rules-based order is much worse.

Sustainable Ideologies for Science

Individualism, and its offshoots, are useful in the beginning, useless after a while, and harmful in the end. Even their opposites—i.e., dissolving everything into oneness, or destroying everything to end with nothingness—are also useful in the beginning, useless after some time, and harmful in the end. This is why we must reject individualism, impersonalism, and voidism equally.

The correct ideology is inseparability, or what we can call unity in diversity and diversity in unity. It is not individualism because there is unity. It is not impersonalism because there is diversity. And it is not voidism because there is both unity and diversity. It is pervasively true and it is sustainable.

Sustainability comes from the fact that this ideology reconciles all dualisms. For example, the individual is inside a collection, and the collection is inside the individual. The collection is not physically inside the individual; rather, the collection is *intentionally* inside the individual—the individual works for the collective good. Likewise, the mind is in the body, and the body is in the mind. The body is in the mind because the body is an idea, but it is only those ideas that we can perceive as sensations; those, however, are not the only ideas; there are other ideas too that are only in the mind. The mind is in the body because those ideas that we cannot perceive shape the body; our bodies are the results of mixing our memories, goals, and consequences. All the parts of a chair are within the chair, and chairness is present in all the parts. People are living inside a culture, and culture is living inside people. Everything is in God, and God is in everything. The parts are in the whole, and the whole is in the parts.

This is not a difficult philosophy. But it is difficult for the individualists, impersonalists, and voidists. It is not unscientific gibberish.

It applies to a rational and empirical study of every subject. In fact, we reach these conclusions after analyzing the problems with all the alternatives. It solves all problems of these subjects created by myriad and never-ending dualisms.

The world is presently ruled by individualists, impersonalists, and voidists. The individualists want to divide the world into independent parts to model and control them. The impersonalists want to unite the world by dissolving all diversity and differences. And the voidists want to destroy both unity and diversity to end up with nothing—essentially ending all conscious experience.

Under the predominance of individualism, impersonalism, and voidism, the most sustainable philosophy finds few friends. It mostly has enemies, critics, competitors, detractors, hecklers, opponents, and rivals. The enemies want to destroy it. The critics say that it is not scientific. The competitors want to win by louder propaganda. The detractors say it seems logically contradictory. The hecklers demand evidence of its truth and question why it is not more popular. The opponents want to peddle individualism, impersonalism, and voidism. And rivals envy its intrinsic beauty and irrefutability. The fact is that this philosophy exists only for the most sincere people. Those are rare. Even though it is the best philosophy ever, it will be accepted only by the thoroughly honest.

Chicken and Egg Problems in Science

The Origin of Chicken-and-Egg Problems

Numerous chicken and egg problems arise while trying to construct the notions of space, time, and objects. For instance, when distance is defined in terms of a meter, then the extension of the meter depends on space and space depends on the meter. Likewise, when duration is defined in terms of a clock, then time must elapse before a clock can move, but the movement of the clock defines the passing of time. Similarly, when concepts are defined in terms of concepts, then objects must preexist concepts but they cannot exist unless the concept exists prior.

I will use this article to elaborate on these problems and then illustrate how they are solved in Sāñkhya philosophy. The conclusion of that discussion is that whatever we call the "body" springs out of a succession of imperceivable realities that are logically necessary for a perceivable world to exist. They are however ignored in modern science leading to unsolved chicken-and-egg problems. These unsolved problems, however, don't disappear from science by neglecting them. They reappear in other places in science and become unsolvable.

Platonic World and Gödel's Incompleteness

Ordinary Object vs. Property Distinction

Let's start with the notion of space. In our common ways of speaking about space, we treat it as an *object* with a *property* called distance. Descartes called space an extended substance, which means that there is a substance with the property of extension. Others have treated space as a container which also means that there is an object with an extension. The problem is that extension is not just in space; everything in space is also extended. Modern science calls some of these things meters. But the meter is not the *definition* of distance, because even if the meter disappeared, distances would not. We will then use another standard, such as a foot, to measure distance, but it would still not be the definition of distance.

Since everything in space is extended, therefore, everything has the property of distance. The property that exists in space, meters, and feet must transcend them because designating one thing as that property's definition entails that its absence must dissolve the property. By transcendence, I mean that distance must be prior to space, meters, and feet and must therefore exist outside space, meters, and feet. But how can we know something outside space? How does something outside space become immanent in space and things in space?

Platonic vs. Set-Theoretic Conception of Number

The transcendence of the concept of distance, and its immanence in space and meters, can be taken to mean that "distance" is a Platonic idea that incarnates in this world to create extended things. However, the incarnation of a Platonic idea into a material world suggests that an idea-like reality precedes an object-like world. This claim is disliked by all materialists. Therefore, science has tried to minimize this problem by saying that every length or extension in turn comprises points, which are in turn numbers, and all numbers are eternally real.

Thereby, distance reduces to infinitesimal points, which then reduces to numbers, but we cannot reduce it further unless we can generate all numbers from a smaller set of numbers, preferably just one. That, unfortunately, has proven to be impossible. Hence, at present, the word "number" denotes not a Platonic idea, but a set of subsets called "real numbers", "rational numbers", "positive integers", "negative integers", "fractions", and so on, which in turn comprise many numbers. By a set-theoretic construction, "number" follows (rather than precedes) the subsets called real, rational, integral, and fractional numbers. Each of these follows (rather than precedes) its members.

Factually, the problem of Platonic ideas is not resolved by set-theoretic constructions because to make a set of "real numbers" we must define what we mean by "real number" to preclude the inclusion of horses and trees in that set. Since we cannot define "number", therefore, we rely on an intuitive grasp of numbers to construct sets such as "real numbers". As a result, there are two incongruent notions of number: (a) the set of elements, and (b) the concept that allows us to see something in each element to qualify it for inclusion in the set.

Attempts to construct all numbers from a few numbers (such as 0 and 1) have failed because they are treated as sets and whichever way we want to define a set (such as a pair of brackets) assumes more than the few numbers (for instance, an empty set {} requires us to define two brackets before we can define zero). Thereby, we neither have a bottoms-up construction of all numbers from few numbers nor do we have a top-down construction of all numbers from "number". Arithmetic has no foundation because "number" has no foundation.

Mathematics talks about numbers as if they were real things. But mathematics doesn't know how to construct these numbers. Numbers are just facts of life. Likewise, length or distance is just a fact of life. We don't try to define "length" because it suffers from the same problem as trying to define "number". We just treat length as a fact of life, pick an arbitrary object called a meter and use it to measure length. Someone else can pick something else. The word "length" just means whatever I want it to mean, by picking some arbitrary standard.

Problems Caused By Set-Theoretic Constructions

Set-theoretic constructions create many other problems. For example, consider the sentence "even number is divisible by two". What do we mean by "even number"? The answer, based on the above attempt to evade the existence of Platonic concepts, is that "even number" is the name of a set. Okay, then "even number" can be partitioned into two sets such as {2, 6, 10, 14, …} and {4, 8, 12, 16, …} and this division of the set into two sets should be the meaning of even number divided by two. But if we take that approach, then "odd number is divisible by two" would also be true, because we can partition the set "odd number" into two sets such as {1, 5, 9, 13, …} and {3, 7, 11, 15, …}.

We can try to solve the problem by rephrasing these claims and we will transform it into another problem. For instance, let's consider the sentence "an even number is divisible by two" where "an even number" is a member of "even numbers". By this definition, the sentence "an odd number is divisible by two" would be false. However, in saying so, we have lost the ability to apply the divisibility claims to sets. For instance, "even numbers are divisible by two" is true, and "odd numbers are divisible by two" is false, for set members. However, both claims are true for the set. How do we know which claim applies to members or sets? We don't. Therefore, to avoid making a false claim about "odd numbers", we must also not make true claims about "even numbers" by excluding "odd numbers" and "even numbers" from discourse.

Problems Caused By Gödel's Incompleteness

This problem is called Gödel's Incompleteness. It results from the fact that the word "even number" can mean both a collection of numbers and an individual member of that collection, quite like 'President' sometimes means a class of individuals and at other times an individual. The sentence "President is tall" may be true for some presidents, but not for all. When someone says "President is tall" we automatically know this to be a claim about a specific person, and not about the class of individuals. But we cannot make that distinction in mathematics.

To prove anything at all, we have to give one definition to "even number" and whichever definition is chosen, either proves false claims or does not prove true claims. Hence, Gödel's Incompleteness says: "Any axiomatic system about numbers must be either inconsistent or incomplete". A system is inconsistent if it proves some false claims. A system is incomplete if it doesn't prove some true claims.

This problem could be solved by rejecting the set-theoretic meaning of "odd number" and "even number" and relying only on Platonic concepts, such as "number", "odd number" and "even number". If the need arises, we can use terms like "the set of odd numbers" and "the set of even numbers" to refer to a collection of numbers. But it would require us to define "number" a priori, derive odd and even numbers from the concept of "number", and then construct individual numbers from these definitions. But we haven't been able to do that because we don't like to accept (owing to materialism) pure concepts such as "number" that must reside outside the material world.

Factually, sets are dispensable, but Platonic concepts are not. Similarly, space, distance, and point are Platonic concepts, and individual spaces, distances, and points are instantiations of these Platonic forms. The foundation of mathematics lies in constructing a Platonic hierarchy of forms, deriving lower-level concepts from higher-level concepts. If we cannot do that, then mathematics has no foundation. Since nobody knows how to create a foundation for mathematics based on Platonic forms, therefore, mathematics has no foundation. The result is that we cannot distinguish between universals and particulars because they pertain to different worlds but under materialism, we have just one world. Materialism, under which a Platonic world of ideas is rejected, leads to the problem of Gödel's Incompleteness.

The Chicken-and-Egg Problem of Space

The "Space Equals Distance" Claim

With set-theoretic problems, distance is an other-worldly Platonic concept, while meter and space are this-worldly instances of that concept. Since there is a universal Platonic world of ideas, therefore, we can still say that "distance" has a universal meaning. However, since nobody can agree on that universal meaning, therefore, we have to defer to our individual notions of "distance". The mind enters mathematics because mathematics resurrects the Platonic world of pure ideas, which nobody can find. We still need to use concepts in science.

We can treat our minds as "this-worldly" and personal notions of "distance" as varied incarnations of the "other-worldly" Platonic idea. This view, however, leads us to three worlds, namely, matter, mind, and mathematics. The mathematical notion of distance in the Platonic world is now reflected in our minds and in material objects, and the objective foundation of mathematics is based on a pure idea of distance, imperfectly known by the human mind and imperfectly applied to the measurement of the distance between material things.

A practical illustration of this problem is that I can look into a microscope and see things bigger than seen by the naked eye. There are two ways of measurement—one by the naked eye and the other through a microscope—that give different results. These results are produced by choosing different standards of length, that differ in what we mean by length. Based on these methods, we can produce different values of length. If someone accepts our standards, then they can obtain the same experiences. But if they reject our choice, their experiences are different. Thereby, length is neither a subjective nor an objective property. It is not purely subjective because someone else can agree with my standard. It is not purely objective property because someone else may not agree with my standard. Our experience is the result of a choice of a standard applied to some reality. Therefore, it is not reality. It is an effect of the combination of subjective and objective.

Thus, no measured distance can be called reality because the world looks bigger through a microscope than through the naked eye, and we don't know what the "true length" is. Thereby, there is some observed length and there is some reality, but they are not the same. In fact, what we observe as length depends on our method of measurement, quite different from a universal Platonic definition of length, and quite distinct from objective length. The distinction between the Platonic world, the mind, and the real world is necessary.

The "Space Does Not Equal Distance" Claim

We solve the problems resulting from the non-objectivity of measured length by calling some length an illusion while another length a reality—e.g., we might say that the lengths seen through a microscope are illusions and those seen by the naked eye are reality. But these are unjustifiable ***metaphysical assertions***. They arise because we try to eliminate the role of the mind in an observation to arrive at some objective reality. Such an objective reality is arbitrarily concocted by deeming a specific measurement method the definition of reality.

There would be no problem in accommodating all these alternative versions of length if the differences were attributed to the choice of different procedures of measurement of the same property. The mind will now enter an objective reality by defining what we "mean" by "distance" by defining how we want to measure the distance. It can include the naked eye and microscopes of varying resolutions. After all, who is to say that only the human naked eye defines the objective measure of spatial length, while the microscope does not?

The "Space is Prior to Distance" Claim

Einstein's theory of special relativity took this problem of the relativity of different observations up a notch when it spoke of observed facts of "length contraction" and "time dilation" even with the same standard of measurement. Different observers can now measure the distance using the same standard and obtain different values. The problem of distance is disputable if we use two different standards to measure distance. But it becomes indisputable when the same standard is used. Now, we must say that distance is just observation.

We can no longer say that space is an objective reality that exists prior to our measurement of distance because no two observers agree on what distance is. The claim works only if we can designate a special observer whose privileged observations define reality. The equivalence of all observers entails that any discussion of "space" or even objective length is metaphysics. The sustainable view is that all measured distances are facts even if observers disagree about them. There is hence no "space". There are just varying distances.

The "Distance is Prior to Space" Claim

After Einstein formulated the theory of special relativity, he also adopted a Kantian stance in which space, time, object, causality, etc. are mere "goggles" through which we see the world rather than objective realities. Thereby, what we see is the combined effect of some external reality and some goggles. The fact that we cannot talk about an objective space or distance is because the distance is not "out there". It is "in me". Space, time, object, or causality may still exist in reality. But there is no way to know what those things in reality are.

Einstein's difference with Kant was that everyone need not have the same standard of distance, even if they call it by the same name. My "meter" need not be the same as yours, although we both call it a "meter". The word "meter" is a pointless label if they are not the same. By applying this concept to perceptions, we construct an external world, including that this world exists in some space. However, space has no external reality. It is rather a conceptual construct based on my chosen, private, and not identical to others', conception of length.

This upgraded Kantian stance relies on a mind-body distinction in which my goggles are separate from reality. The problem is that these "goggles" are equated to measuring instruments, which are also in space. Hence, instead of being the goggles through which we see reality, they become the reality being seen. Instead of being pure concepts, they become the individual things being seen. When a property is defined using a measuring instrument (instead of a Platonic concept) the result is that there are infinite arbitrary definitions of such properties. Due to the fact that the two observers haven't derived their concept of distance from a Platonic idea, they simply cannot agree on the property.

This is another outcome of materialism, namely, if we reject a common Platonic reference then there is no reference. We cannot say that "the object is five meters in length" is an objectively false statement because for all we know it could be true for some particular observer whose "meter" has been elongated or shortened to make that claim true, although it is not true for other observers. Each observer is an axiomatic reference frame in which each word has a different meaning, (a) some true claims based on a chosen axiomatic framework are unprovable due to Gödel's Incompleteness, (b) but claims true for another axiomatic framework may be false in our chosen axiomatic framework. Since no axiomatic framework is preferred over another, therefore, everything is true for some observers and false for others.

The Solution to the Chicken-and-Egg Problem

The Construction of an Experienced World

We are led to the chicken-and-egg problem because (a) "distance" has two meanings—conceptual and physical, and only one of those could be used in an axiomatic framework as a result of Gödel's Incompleteness, (b) each observer can redefine their conceptual and physical notions differently making different claims true, false, and unprovable, (c) there is no objective truth due to these arbitrarily chosen definitions, (d) because science works, therefore, we must suppose that there is some objective truth although none of these positions can be called a privileged truth because there is no universal observer, and (e) privileged truth must be tied only to a universal observer.

The solution to the problem of relativization requires us to say that there is a "pure" concept of distance but each observer may have an "impure" concept of distance produced by modifying the "pure" concept through some mechanism. The pure and impure concepts of distance are prior to the space of objects. They exist uniquely in each observer's mind as the subjective concepts of "near" and "far". These varied notions of "near" and "far" are then converted into the choice of a measuring instrument such that (a) an observer with an impure idea longer than the pure idea of distance uses a longer unit of measurement (such as a meter) and (b) an observer with an impure idea shorter than the pure idea of distance uses a shorter unit of measurement (such as a foot). The choice of measuring instruments is subjective but not arbitrary. It is also rooted in our personal notions of "near" and "far" or "long" and "short". Once the measurement standard is chosen, it is used for measuring distances. However, these standards are not fixed.

As an observer moves, the standards keep changing. Therefore, the outcome of measurement can be called an observer-centric *fact*, but it cannot be called an observer-independent *truth*.

The choice of what we mean by "near" and "far", which we have called an impurity above, is itself driven by a complicated subjective process involving emotions, intentions, cognitions, conations, and relations. A little distance from those we love seems far. A great distance from those whom we hate seems not so far. The outcome you desire seems near when you feel optimistic and far when you feel pessimistic. Something big seems not so big in the context of bigger things and something small seems not so small in the context of smaller things. A small achievement of a loved one seems big but a big achievement of an unrelated person seems small. What we focus on gets bigger and what we defocus on gets smaller. In this way, there is a very complex process by which "big" and "small", or "near" and "far", keep changing. The problem of changing notions of length and distance is not confined to observers. It can be extended even to instruments.

Relativistic theories confine change to "speed" and "acceleration" and by such confinement, a wider variety of changing notions of distances are disregarded. But even within this confined notion of change, we can see that distance is just a fact and not a truth. To get to the truth, we have to talk about a pure concept of distance, followed by various modifications of that distance based on varied personal factors. The facts we see, or how the world appears to us, isn't the truth if the pure concepts have been modified in various ways. That doesn't mean there isn't truth. It just means that we cannot know that truth unless we talk about pure and impure concepts. The world we perceive is constructed by combining the pure and impure. If the impurity is removed, and the purity remains, then the observed facts become the truth.

The Role of Distance in Sāñkhya Philosophy

Returning to the problem of standard selection, we select a standard such as a meter based upon the personal conceptual notion of "near" and "far". Sāñkhya explains how conceptual "near" and "far" become a meter. The basic principle is that our personal notion of near and far creates the smallest distinction we can perceive through our senses. That personal notion translates into the smallest perceivable distinctions between tones, pitches, pushes, textures, colors, shapes, flavors, and smells, and defines the refinement of the senses. What we call a "unit length" is one aspect of *our vision* that corresponds to the smallest distance we can obtain perceptually, akin to a millimeter.

The *objectively* smallest length corresponds to the senses of an observer with the most refined sense perception. That observer is Nature. Her notion of "small" defines the objectively smallest atom; nobody can measure a distance smaller than that. In Vedic cosmology, there are many universes within the material creation that vary in the level of refinement. Hence, the smallest measurable distance—that defines the "atomic" unit of distance—is different for different universes. The present universe has the least variety, which means the coarsest capacity for discrimination. The smallest measurable length—the atomic unit of length—is the biggest for our universe among all universes.

Different species of life within a universe have different levels of coarser or finer discriminations. Each species is incapable of perception smaller than its capacity to discriminate. For instance, even if particle physics measures subatomic particles using powerful accelerators and detectors, the measurements have to be brought to the level of the human sense perception—e.g., a hearable click or a visible dot. Thereby, we think we are perceiving subatomic particles, but we are only perceiving clicks and dots. We *infer* these clicks and dots into the existence of subatomic particles, but there are infinite other inferences that could be drawn from the same clicks and dots, due to which we can never be sure of what the subatomic reality is. True knowledge would require us to have discrimination as fine as the subatomic particle.

The Personalist Nature of Semantic Atomism

A musician has a refined sense of hearing because he can distinguish small tone and pitch differences. A chef has a refined sense of taste and smell because he can distinguish minor differences between tastes and smells. An artist has a refined sense of sight because he can distinguish minor differences in color shades. A writer has a refined grasp of the language by which he uses specific synonyms to describe different things. This refinement in sensual and mental perception depends on a person's personal notion of atomism.

The smallest click we can hear and the smallest dot we can see is the *atom* for us. In Sāñkhya, it is called a *trisarenu*—the smallest dust particles we can see in the light pouring through a window. That *trisarenu* is in turn comprised of three dyads or six aspects—the six aspects are called *paramānu*, the three dyads are called *anu*, and the combination of three dyads is called a *trisarenu*. These six aspects are subdivisions of cognition, namely, a percept, a concept, three kinds of judgments—true, right, and good—and finally an individual.

Even as we perceive a "dust particle", some of us may try to imagine "What it is to be like a dust particle?" They might find the existence desirable or not. Almost nobody wonders if the movement of such a dust particle is actually a righteous or unrighteous activity, although such a judgment could also be made. Accordingly, the percept is the easiest cognition, the concept of a dust particle is the next cognition, that these dust particles are not my hallucination is the next harder cognition, that being such a thing would be good is the next harder cognition, and that this existence also performs a necessary and righteous role in the universe is the hardest of all these cognitive conclusions.

Consciousness Converts Concepts to Percepts

Concepts and percepts underdetermine each other. The concept table underdetermines the percepts because tables can be of varied shapes and sizes. Likewise, a shape and size can be variously called a table or a chair. Similarly, the concept of "small" is underdetermined unless "small" is qualified by a tone, pitch, push, texture, color, shape, size, color, flavor, or smell. What seems a small change in tone to a tone-deaf person will not be small for others. A tone-deaf person may have an advanced sense of smell, that can detect minor changes in odor. Thereby, "small" is not fixed even for the same person. The word "small" has different meanings for "small tone change" and "small smell change".

We can illustrate this by asking: What do we *mean* by "small"? The first answer is: It is found in a small variation in tone. Then we can ask: What do we *mean* by a "small variation in tone". The second answer is: It is found in a small pressure. Then we can ask: What do we *mean* by a "small pressure"? The third answer is: It is found in a small movement. This is how we explain "small" via *examples*. Sound, touch, sight, taste, and smell are just examples of "small". Since they are examples, therefore, "small" is *in* the examples. But since these are just examples, therefore, "small" is not *confined* to these examples. We must say that "small" is both immanent in and transcendent to its examples.

This expansion of the concept into its examples will not arise unless there is someone asking the question: What is the meaning of X? Hence, a concept expands into its examples only under the presence of consciousness. Sāñkhya merely states that a subtle reality expands into a gross reality under the presence of consciousness. Nyāya however explains the role of consciousness in causing that expansion in greater detail. That process is trying to overcome the underdetermination by asking questions. An object cannot ask questions. A person can. Those who study Sāñkhya purely as a material theory can never explain this expansion in Sāñkhya because even as "small" is incompletely defined without its examples, that incompleteness exists only if there is a person to consider it incomplete and try to complete it.

The cause of incompleteness is called *abhāva* or absence in Nyāya. Consciousness experiences an absence and triggers a material expansion. If this consciousness is withdrawn, then the examples of "small" merge into the original concept of "small". Similarly, the fact that "small" manifests only into sound, touch, sight, taste, and smell, is also due to the fact that incompleteness is overcome by these five-fold illustrations. Since there are no more questions, therefore, there are no more answers and expansions. For instance, if someone asked "What do you mean by small?" and the answer was given in terms of something that can never be perceived, then it would not be considered a useful illustration or example. Hence, even as Sāñkhya is a theory of matter, it is inextricably tied to the nature of consciousness.

Objective and Subjective Property Difference

The Notion of Distance and Space Revisited

To recapitulate, distance and space are not identical; distance is prior to space. Distance is a subjective concept indicated by—(a) we cannot perceive something smaller than a select distance, (b) we consider different things to be smaller or bigger based on personal ideas, (c) these personal ideas of small and big evolve with time, (d) the changing notions of big and small alter our standards and then the perceived reality is pictured as bigger or smaller in our experience. And yet, because this subjective concept is constructed from an objectively smallest distance, therefore, "atomic length" is an objective concept. But it is not *our* concept; it is Nature's perceptual ability, which means that there is something in Nature that can detect the "atomic length" and magnify it into a "measurable length" that humans can perceive. Seeing that magnified length is not the same as seeing atomic length. Thereby, there is no conflict between the subjective and the objective lengths.

The fact that there is objective length doesn't mean that we can divorce length from perception. Length is not *defined* by a meter or foot, although length is immanent in both meter and foot. Length is rather a transcendent property, instantiated as one of the examples of the concept "small". The mental concept of "small" initially appears as the definition of small in terms of the sense of seeing (a measurement procedure), and then transforms into a visible object that we perceive by sight as small based on our sensual or mental concepts.

Likewise, the concept of "distance" is created by establishing a relationship between things. We can be near or far from small or big things; hence, smallness and nearness are not identical. Smallness pertains to an object while nearness pertains to a relationship with an object. They are distinct as cognition and relation. However, due to the use of modalities—i.e., the possibility of using the same word in many ways—we can equate smallness to nearness in some cases although not in others. For instance, we can see a forest as a small patch of green. In this case, a big thing is seen as small due to our distance from it. The factual bigness is an objective property of the forest. But due to our distant relationship, it seems small. Thus, nearness and smallness are not identical. And yet, you can sometimes say nearness is a small distance.

All length measurements are thus subjective properties although there is an objective reality. The same thing can seem bigger or smaller to us, based on our relation to it. The perceived size and distance constitute our perceptual space, distinct from the objective reality. Thus, what we measure as space or observe as a "world" is not reality. It is an appearance of reality. But there is a reality, not identical to the observed fact. Facts are not reality. Rather, facts are byproducts of the interaction between our perceptual apparatus and reality.

Bridgman's Operationalist View of Science

The distinction between fact and reality cannot be overcome by using measuring instruments. One of the clearest illustrations of this problem comes from the fact that we cannot devise a measuring instrument that can effectively measure both small and big. For instance, the scale that weighs trucks cannot be used to weigh diamond jewelry accurately, and vice versa. We have to use two separate scales and we cannot calibrate them. This intuitively trivial problem was demonstrated by P. W. Bridgman in his measurement of gas pressures.

Bridgman found that the pressure gauges that worked for small pressures did not work for big pressures. The gauge for low pressures would break down when subjected to high pressures. New gauges had to be devised for different pressure ranges, which led to the problem of calibrating the gauges relative to other gauges. The problem with calibrating the gauges is that the lower-pressure gauges produce erroneous results near the top end of their pressure ranges, while the higher-pressure gauges produce erroneous results near the bottom end of their pressure ranges. That is just like you will not get the accurate weight of diamond jewelry using a scale that is meant to weigh trucks. So, how are you going to calibrate the low- and high-pressure gauges if you aren't sure if the measuring instrument is giving us accurate results?

Bridgman got so flustered with this problem that he formulated a philosophy of Operationalism in which there is no meaning to a property like "pressure" other than the value given by a specific gauge that cannot be guaranteed to be calibrated with other gauges. If a gauge says that the pressure is 10 pounds per square inch, there is no way to know if this is 100 times the gauge that indicates a pressure of 0.1 pounds per square inch. All attempts to calibrate gauges suffer from this problem. Hence, we cannot know the deviation between gauges. Bridgman concluded: There is no meaning to "pressure" than *my* current instrument. In short, science is not about objective facts if those require an extended scale because there is no universal scale and instruments cannot be calibrated. We use these numbers in approximate theoretical models although the models don't match the data perfectly. We don't know if the model is wrong or if our measurements are.

The problem magnifies by orders of magnitude when we talk about small values in terms of larger scales. For example, there is no meaning to a value like 10^{-20} meters because we need to calibrate 20 different length scales to operate across 20 different orders of length magnitude and we cannot. If our theory rests on finding precise values and the instruments are imprecise, we have no hope. Although Bridgman won a Nobel Prize in physics, he was attacked due to the implied pessimism of his conclusion. Eventually, he gave up trying to explain the problem, the noise died, and everyone happily went back to studying the nature of "objective reality" in science through the use of instruments.

The Problem of Measurement in Science

Of course, to uphold any realism, Bridgman's conclusion that "pressure" means a gauge should mean that the gauge is contained inside the gas whose pressure was being measured. This is the only way to say that gas *has* pressure. Since this conclusion is also untenable, therefore, to be perfectly consistent, we have to say that there is no such thing as pressure. Rather, some gas in contact with some gauge shows us some pointer values. But we cannot formulate a scientific theory with such an interpretation of scientific measurements. Any kind of realism requires us to suppose that "pressure" is a Platonic idea, which constitutes the smallest measurable unit of pressure in Nature. Instruments commonly used by humans use variable multiples of the natural unit but without the natural standard, we cannot calibrate them.

Hence, if an experiment concludes that a theoretically calculated value has been detected, there are huge assumptions involved—the gauge that measured this value was perfectly calibrated with all the other gauges that were previously used to measure all other values in all the other experiments. That calibration does not exist, and it is impossible to achieve it. A gauge could behave differently in a hot environment vs. a cold one. To accurately measure pressure, we have to align the temperatures. But the temperature gauge can also depend on the pressure in the environment. These cyclical interdependencies between various properties preclude any reliable instrument calibration.

The problem never disappears. It gets more complicated as we consider more properties. For instance, to measure time using a clock, we have to define the distance between two points on a clock. If that distance expands or contracts, then the measured value of time is meaningless. In this process, time depends on space. Likewise, if we are trying to measure distance by roundtripping a light beam, what we conclude as distance depends on how much time it took the light to roundtrip. In this case, the distance value depends on time. The clock that measures time can go slower or faster based on ambient pressure and temperature. To measure temperature using a thermometer, or pressure using a gauge, we have to be sure that the scales that indicate the numerical value on these gauges are not expanding or contracting.

All real-world measurements of properties are so inextricable from every other property that we can never be sure that the value we are measuring is a property of the world and not the measurement instrument playing tricks on the observer. The pointer movement can never be attributed to one property. Instead, we have to say that this pointer moves so much, under the condition that all the other property pointers moved so much, and all these pointers are somehow mutually entangled but not identical to any other pointer elsewhere.

This general problem of inextricability is called Bhedābheda in Vedic philosophy, which means distinct but inseparable. The measurement of time, space, temperature, pressure, mass, charge, or any other property conceived in science, is *inextricable* from the measurement of every other property. All these properties are aspects of reality and change to one aspect can change all other properties. When properties are thus inextricable, then we cannot add or multiply these properties as if they were independent variables. That is the end of using mathematics to study nature, which relies on the assumption that the variables involved in a scientific equation are independent of each other.

The Logical Necessity of Truthful Laws

The empirical method of science is deeply flawed due to the assumptions of separability. The correct method is a logical necessity that has to be established prior to observation. If the observation varies from a logically necessary truth, then variations must be attributed to the observer's impurity. This method is employed in Nyāya. Just because we don't see some reality doesn't falsify its truth. Just because we perceive something other than the logically necessary truth, doesn't falsify the truth. The absence of evidence is not evidence of absence. The variation of evidence is not evidence of variation. The presence of evidence is not evidence of presence. We might just be hallucinating a presence, when it doesn't exist. We might be modifying reality while perceiving it. Or we may not perceive the reality that exists.

Observation is neither necessary nor sufficient to guarantee the truth if our mental and sensual instruments are flawed. The inability to validate a logically necessary theory doesn't invalidate the theory. It rather calls for perfecting the perceptual capacity. Such a process is called the *purification of consciousness*. Meanwhile, before we pursue the purification of consciousness, we can become convinced of the truth based on a logical necessity. It involves seeking answers to questions such as—Does space equal distance? Does space not equal distance? Is distance prior to space? Is space prior to distance? Logical necessity rests on eliminating alternatives by reasoning.

When all that is impossible has been eliminated, then whatever remains, however improbable, is true. Most people are not convinced by the correctness of the improbable because they have not eliminated the impossible. They may have taken the existence of space for granted without asking if distance came before space or space came before distance. For them, the truth of the idea that space emerged out of the mind seems improbable because they haven't yet examined the problem of distance. Hence, philosophy has a role in eliminating the impossible. It is the path—prior to the purification to consciousness—to accept the improbable. Once we are convinced about the improbable, we have to realize it by perception too. But that process can take time as it requires us to perfect the instruments of perception.

Other Chicken-and-Egg Problems in Science

Fundamental Problem of Time Measurement

The detailed discussion of the problem involved in measuring the property of length can be generalized to all kinds of measurements. We have already discussed such problems with pressure and temperature. But the issue is not limited to these properties. The problems pervade all fundamental concepts. We will now turn our attention to the illustration of these problems for other types of concepts.

Time, like space, involves a conundrum: Did duration come before time or did time come before duration? The measurement of duration generally involves a clock. But for the fingers of a clock to move, time must elapse. The passing of time can move the fingers of a clock, which we can then measure as duration. The clock fingers can move slower or faster, which means everyone can have a different clock and conclude that different durations must have elapsed. Our personal notions of long and short durations, however, depend on some objective passing of time. What is the meaning of that objective time, different from the measures of duration through different personal clocks?

This problem is also solved in Vedic philosophy by describing a Causal Time. It is the choice to make the smallest amount of change defined by Nature. Time appears to pass because—(a) there is a succession of choices that make a change, and (b) each choice involves an atomic duration. Atomic time is the duration involved in making an atomic change by an atomic choice. Since atomic change can vary across universes, hence, the smallest measurable durations also vary across universes. We cannot measure a time smaller than atomic time because measurements require something to change, and the smallest change cannot occur without the passing of atomic time.

Time must pass before a duration can be measured. Hence, distance is prior to space, but time is prior to duration. Atomic time is also a choice just like atomic distance. Science has never understood time. It cannot solve this problem because calculus assumes that time passes. No mathematical theory can answer this question because the answer lies in the role of choice in making an atomic change. Science also cannot explain why time *seems* to go slower or faster, and why some people live longer because their time seems to pass slower to them.

Fundamental Problem of Object Definition

The problem of object definition is seen in set theory. To form a set of horses, one must have the *idea* of a horse before we can identify a horse or add that horse to the set of horses. If we don't have the idea of a horse, then we cannot construct a set of horses. Therefore, even if we try to define the word "horse" as a set, we are still relying on the idea of "horse" as different from a set.

Similarly, to form a set of two things, you must know what "two" means. Otherwise, how will we ensure that the set has two rather than three members? We have to assume that there is a concept of twoness prior to forming the set of two things. And once we form the set of two things, the word "two" acquires two meanings—(a) the set of two things, and (b) the concept of twoness prior to the set. Mathematicians have unsuccessfully tried to evade this problem in many ways. For instance, one such attempt claims that we can define numbers as follows. 0:= {}, 1:= {{}}, 2:= {{}, {{}}}, and so on. Basically, 0 is an empty set; 1 is a set with one member—0; 2 is a set with two members—0 and 1. The question is: How do we represent an empty set? The simplest answer is "two braces". So, to define 0 syntactically, we have to have the notion of 2 prior. To define 1 syntactically, we have to have the notion of 4 prior. This circularity makes all definitions impossible.

Fundamental Problem of Person Definition

There are even more serious issues in defining persons. For instance, if a person is defined as a set of objects, then any change in the set membership must change the person. Just by eating food or drinking water, we would become a different person because the set members have changed. This problem can only be avoided by saying that the person is both transcendent to and immanent in the body. If the person wasn't immanent in the body, then hurting the body would not be hurting the person. If the person wasn't transcendent to the body, then a minor change in the body (such as while hurting it) would change the person. Both properties are required to clearly define personhood.

How can we make a society with laws, property ownership, and rights if we cannot define what a person is? If merely drinking water changes the person, then the property purchased before drinking water is no longer owned after drinking water because the person before and after drinking water is different. Someone can commit a crime and drink water to disown all responsibility for the crime. A person can borrow money from a bank and drink water to deny that he ever borrowed money. Society cannot exist without personhood.

Similarly, unless we recognize a role for a will, a bullet shot by a person with a gun to his head would be attributed not to the person who holds the gun to the head but to the shooter who shot the bullet. If we deny a role for will then the person who did not shoot will go unpunished while the person who shot under coercion will bear full punishment. Laws of a society cannot exist without personhood. But personhood cannot be equated to the body due to the above problems. Hence, a person precedes the existence of a body.

Fundamental Problem of Inanimate Persons

If you buy a car, and you happen to scratch its bumper in an accident, you do not lose ownership of the car just because the material ingredients of the car are no longer what they were when you bought the car. If you buy a house, and you happen to paint it subsequently, you do not lose ownership of the house just because the material ingredients of the house are no longer what they were when you bought it. Houses and cars are given serial numbers to identify them as immutable things even when they are remodeled. That is just like a person remains immutable after eating food and drinking water. We may not ascribe will to houses and cars, and yet, their immutability requires us to treat them just like persons. Similarly, businesses are identified as immutable persons even if they move their offices, hire or fire employees, or change their logos. Cities and countries are identified as immutable persons even when people enter or leave them, even as material resources are moved in and out of them. If a country conquers a territory without changing its constitution, the new territory becomes a part of the original country, quite like a person who eats food or drinks water adds matter to his body without a change in identity.

The problems in defining objects, thus, extend to defining persons, and those problems then reflect back into the definition of personal property ownership. The problems of property ownership inherit the problems of both personhood and object definition. Unless this general problem of property ownership is solved, the problem of object definition cannot be fully solved. Since the object definition relies on the definition of space and time, therefore, we have to solve the problem of will and time, then the problem of space, then the problem of objects, and then the problem of ownership of objects which are within space and time although the person willing it is outside space and time.

Numerous Mediocrities of Materialism

Materialism has no answer to these problems. There is no understanding of the problems in trying to define space, time, and objects. There is no understanding of the problems in defining persons and property ownership. The problems of defining space, time, and objects constitute a limited domain of truth. The problems of personhood constitute a limited domain of good. And the problems of property ownership constitute a limited domain of rightness. If we can solve these problems simultaneously, then we can solve the problems of truth, right, and good. However, since no materialistic theory solves these problems, therefore, there is no truth, right, or good within materialism.

Materialism substitutes answers to deep questions about the origins of space, time, and objects with the axiomatization of their existence. Materialism is a morally inadequate doctrine that cannot answer the most basic questions of why a person without choice must be rewarded or punished. Materialism is an emotionally sterile doctrine that substitutes a life of great purpose with one of surviving without purpose.

Materialism is popular among the zombies who do not inquire into deep questions about reality, are not interested in developing moral character, and are unable to think of anything beyond day-to-day existence. Or, perhaps, they are incapable of such things which they rationalize by calling them non-existent or impossible. Materialism is a philosophy of the zombies, by the zombies, and for the zombies. It is also a philosophy of the mediocre, by the mediocre, and for the mediocre. It is an intellectual rationalization of mediocrity.

The mediocre are relieved if they don't have to find the truth, do their moral duties, or lead a purposeful life. An ideology that denies the possibility of truth, right, and good unburdens the mediocre person from the guilt of not knowing the truth, right, and good, and not even trying to seek it. Materialism is that sedative that suppresses the last remnant of remorse a mediocre person may feel while comparing themselves to earnest people. Of course, since mediocrity has always existed, hence, materialism has always existed. But when it becomes a prominent dogma in society, we must understand that most of society is mediocre and getting quite comfortable with mediocrity.

The Illusion of Space, Time, and Motion

The Description of the World as Māyā

Modern science emerged from the distinction between space, time, and motion. It required the space, time, and motion to be continuous and smooth, which were formulated as axioms in calculus. The concepts of continuity and smoothness in calculus are false because bodies (such as our hands) can move discontinuously and unsmoothly (e.g., while writing some text).

Continuity and disrecreteness, however, are simultaneously true properties of consciousness. Each choice is discrete but the person who makes that choice is continuous. Due to continuity, the choices of a person are rewarded and punished long after the choice causing them is over.

The ideas of continuous and smooth space, time, and motion has became a hindrance to the resolution of quantized and relativized notions of reality and observation. Such problems, however, do not arise if continuity and discreteness are assigned to consciousness.

In this article, I will discuss how the *illusion* of Newtonian space, time, and motion is created due to sense perception and instrument measurement, while the *reality* is three types of distances, durations, and changes—conceptual, relational, and emotional. I have discussed this before, however, when the issue is complex, more discussion can only benefit it.

Due to the illusion of a Newtonian or Euclidean space and time, the material world is called māyā in all Vedic texts. Cosmology, by comparison, is described in a few texts, and always after the world is called māyā. Thus, māyā is not just the more pervasive name for the world but always prior to cosmology. Under the influence of māyā, what is quite near may appear to be quite far and what is quite far may appear to be quite near. Of the many kinds of adverse effects of māyā, distance is one. Decluttering the meaning of distance is therefore essential before we discuss Vedic cosmology. Without it, Vedic cosmology is incomprehensible.

The Mechanism for Creating Illusions

Imagine there are two computers—A and B—that exchange messages with each other. Each message contains three things—(a) the addresses of the source and destination computers, (b) a type of property, and (c) a value of the property. For instance, a message can be: "My size is 10". Here, "my" is the address of the message sender, size is the type of property, and 10 is the value of that property. The receiving computer takes the message at face value—i.e., trusts the sender—to conclude that the sender's size is 10.

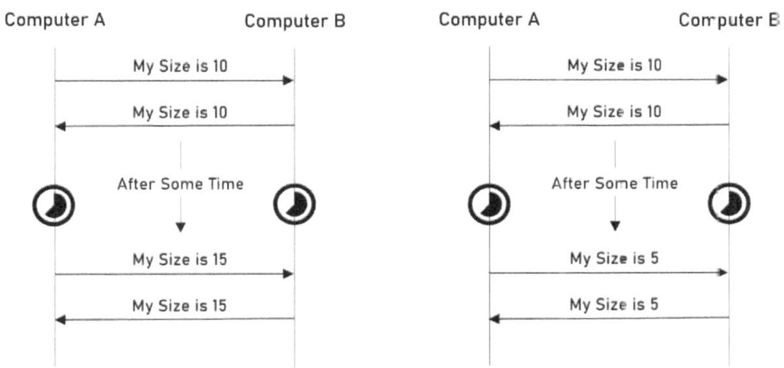

The Illusion of Coming Close

The Illusion of Going Far

If the two computers periodically send the same message to each other, each computer will conclude: The size is unchanged, therefore, the other computer is not moving. So, assume that after some time, one or both of the computers send a different message to each other: "My size is 15". Compared to the previous message, the size has increased, so the receiver will conclude: "The other computer is coming closer to me". If instead, one or both of the computers send a different message to each other: "My size is 5", compared to the previous message, the size has decreased, so the receiver will conclude: "The other computer is going farther from me". The computers aren't moving. But an illusion of motion is created by message exchange as we compare the past and present content of messages, and infer increasing size as decreasing distance, or vice versa.

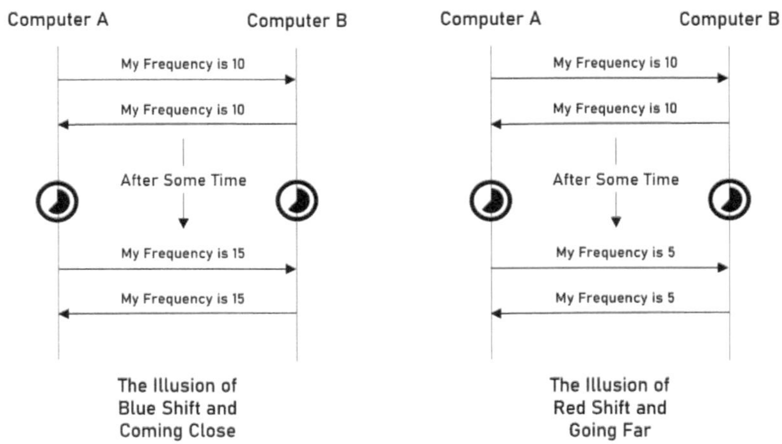

A different method of distance measure is used in modern cosmology by gauging red and blue shifts of light. One party sends a message to the other: "My frequency is 10". If this is constant over time, then the sender is static relative to the receiver. If the message changes to "My frequency is 15", then the sender is moving closer to the receiver, due to a "blue shift" (increased frequency). If the message changes to "My frequency is 5", then the sender is moving farther from the receiver, due to a "red shift" (decreased frequency). The sender and receiver are not moving. But there is an illusion of motion.

Epistemology: Four Defects of Living Entities

In Vedic texts, all living entities are said to have four defects: (a) hallucination, (b) misperception, (c) misinterpretation, and (d) cheating. Each of these four defects can be understood in terms of the above message exchange:

- Hallucination: A sends a message to itself: "B's size is 10" and believes it to be true although B did not send that message. A hallucination of B is created by a self-addressed message.
- Misperception: A receives a message "B's size is 10". But A is using a binary number system instead of a decimal number system. So, A interprets 10 as 2 to conclude: B's size is 2.
- Misinterpretation: The above examples, where we interpret messages with changing property values as the effect of the motion of the sender and receiver, are examples of misinterpretation.
- Cheating: B sends a message to A: "My size is 20" when the size is actually 10. A receives this message, trusts the sender's verdict, and incorrectly concludes: B is twice as big as me.

People sometimes ask: What is Vedic epistemology? The correct answer is—Every living entity in the material world is suffering from hallucinations, misperceptions, misinterpretations, and cheating propensity, which is why the world is called māyā. To understand how the world is māyā, we must use semantics—e.g., that causal interaction is not based on force but on message transfers. The māyā description is different from objective realism of modern science.

Instruments also work based on message exchanges because they too are parts of māyā. Hence, instrument measurements are not better than sense perception. Thus, epistemology is (a) understanding how an illusion is created, (b) the nature of reality as meanings and messages, and (c) the various types of meanings required to exchange messages.

For instance, a message will not be sent deterministically. There has to be some purpose for sending a message. When a message is sent, it may not be sent to everyone; therefore, everyone will not know the existence of everything. The messages sent to different receivers can vary in content and/or periodicity, so when they know, they know it differently and occasionally. A message can be understood only by putting the sender and receiver in a common linguistic convention. Otherwise, the message means one thing, and we think it means something else. The message content can be false, therefore, even sense perception or instrument measurement is not reliable. When sense perception or instrument measurement is elevated to the level of reliable truth then the interpretations that follow are always false.

Meaningful and Purposeful Reality

All messages have many properties—(a) they exist, (b) they have a meaning, (c) the meaning can be false, (d) the truth depends on the linguistic convention, (e) the message is sent for some purpose, (f) the message can be sent to select recipients, (g) messages sent to different recipients can be different, (h) messages sent to different recipients can have variable periodicities, and (i) when the purpose of the senders and the receivers changes, then the content, linguistic convention, truth, periodicity, and recipients can change.

Thereby, a meaningless and purposeless world works differently than a meaningful and purposeful world. The causal mechanisms in a meaningless and purposeless world are not the sources of illusion, but they are the sources of illusion in a meaningful and purposeful world.

Modern science replaces messages with force particles such as photons and gravitons. If the message periodicity changes or the delay between the messages is altered, we attribute these to greater or lesser distances rather than a changing purpose. When the message content changes, we infer these to be the truth, when they can also be false, or merely the result of a changing purpose. When a message is received, we assume that everyone must be receiving the same message. Force particles do not need linguistic conventions while messages do. Thus, a physical conception of reality interacting through forces creates many misconceptions. We measure the length, weight, and speed of a message, ignoring what it means, and whether it is true. By adopting a physical conception, the observers take illusions to be truths.

Therefore, when we substitute the physical concepts of photons and gravitons with messages—and call it semantics—we are trying to explain how the world is māyā. If we don't begin with the basic premise, namely, that the world is māyā, then we cannot explain the four defects of all living entities. However, when we change the conception of reality then the conceptions of space, time, and motion are also illusions. The reality is that a message was received. The illusion is that the content of the message was misinterpreted to create a false notion of space, time, and motion. So, the reality is deluding. The illusion is not comprehended because messages between senders and receivers are replaced with photons and gravitons.

Epistemology Naturally Leads to Ontology

With this understanding of māyā, we get an ontology, namely, that there is a world of senders, receivers, and messages. There is a "distance" between senders and receivers based on:

- What kinds of messages do they send to themselves, receive, and call reality,
- What kinds of messages are they able to receive and parse correctly or incorrectly,
- What kinds of received messages do they trust to be true or distrust to be false,
- What kinds of messages—honest or deceptive—do they prefer to send or receive.

Similarly, there is a conception of "duration" between senders and receivers based on:

- How long it takes them to send messages to themselves and receive them,
- How long it takes them to parse received messages correctly or incorrectly,
- How long it takes them to accept the process of

sending-receiving messages,
- How long it takes them to construct an honest or deceptive message.

Finally, there is a conception of change or "evolution" of the senders and receivers:

- Is their self-sending of messages with varied contents increasing or decreasing?
- Is their parsing of messages with varied types of content improving or worsening?
- Is their judgment of what are trustworthy messages improving or worsening?
- Is their inclination toward honest or deceptive messages increasing or decreasing?

The Philosophy of the Soul and its Delusion

The soul is described as sat-chit-ānanda, which can be described through many trichotomies such as (a) truth, right, and good, (b) logos, ethos, pathos, and (b) rational, emotional, and practical. When māyā covers the soul as its mind and body, then each of these three aspects of the soul is covered to create various kinds of illusions. Therefore, when we study the world in science, we should be studying māyā—(a) the various types of māyā, (b) how māyā that covers also changes with time, and (c) what the soul experiences as a result of māyā.

Based on the above principle of māyā covering the soul, we can divide māyā based on the three aspects of the soul, the three qualities of māyā that cover each of the three aspects of the soul, the changes to these three qualities as evolution, and the time it takes to change the three qualities of māyā to get another kind of māyā. This is how we get space (distance between the different kinds of māyā), time (duration it takes to convert one type of māyā into another), and change (the path that a person follows to go from one type of māyā to another).

Since moving objects are not moving, and yet, seem to be moving due to message exchanges, therefore, Vedic philosophy is not interested in the study of motion. It is only interested in the progressive or regressive paths of the soul. There is an alternative science of change for that.

If at any moment, the soul trusts māyā as truth, he gets attached to the māyā and stops evolving. It continues the process of sending and receiving message of a certain type and considers that motion. However, the soul cannot get out of the universe through such motion. One has to reject one type of māyā and either seek the perfect truth or another kind of māyā. To escape the world of illusion, one has to be skeptical about sense perception itself. With such skepticism, the soul transcends matter. Skepticism of one type of māyā but trust of another, naturally takes the soul from one type of māyā to another. The soul is thus deluded by māyā.

Vedic cosmology presents an understanding of how long the material journey can be. The various parts of the material world are various kinds of māyā. A soul can move from one part of the universe to another, appreciate it more than the previous part of the world, until it rejects all forms of illusions. The illusion can get more enticing and alluring. Different parts of the cosmos offer different kinds of enticements and allurements. We are attracted to these only if we don't remember that this was described as māyā at the outset. This means, that as soon as one is enticed and allured into some māyā, he starts trusting it. That trust will be eventually broken. When it is broken, a person feels cheated and embittered. Therefore, a fair warning is given through cosmology—there are many kinds of māyā, so remain skeptical throughout.

The True Cause of the Material Illusion

Of the four problems of epistemology, cheating is the most fundamental. It arises in the desire to get something without giving something in return, and called *selfishness.* But a person can be honestly or dishonestly selfish. Honest selfishness is beyond the material world and called Brahman. The person who transcends the material world is selfish, but he is not dishonest. In contrast, mostly everyone in the material world is not just selfish but also dishonest.

The material world fundamentally exists to correct the flaw of the cheating propensity in the soul. A cheater is corrected through cheating in precisely those ways (a) that he wants to be cheated or (b) he has been cheating others. The material energy uses misinterpretation, misperception, and hallucination to cheat a person, while each person is trying to cheat another person. Hence, every cheater is cheated by material energy and by other cheaters.

We see something and we interpret it in some way because we want it to be like that. The desire precedes the māyā. We misperceive reality because we want it to be like that. But it is not like that. We hallucinate in some way because we want it to be like that. But it is not like that. The world is māyā or delusion because we have a cheating propensity. It cannot be corrected except by cheating the cheater. Cheating is justice for the cheater.

Thus, even as māyā has three forms—hallucination, misperception, and misinterpretation—they are also secondary outcomes of the primary form of cheating propensity. Western epistemology talks about the secondary problems of hallucination, misperception, and misinterpretation. But no Western academic talks about the primary problem of cheating.

In fact, most people are offended if we say that modern science is cheating. They believe that while doing an academic, scientific, and epistemological discussion, we should only criticize science in terms of hallucination, misperception, and misinterpretation, but never question the motives and integrity of a scientist. But without the primary motive, we can never explain why the secondary effects of hallucination, misperception, and misinterpretation even exist.

Therefore, we have to ask: How did we get into the situation where we have epistemological problems? Why don't we have senses and minds that give us the truth? Why are most people wrong for the most part most of the time in most of the possible ways? What is the reason that we are continuously deceived through hallucination, misperception, and misinterpretation?

Eastern vs. Western Epistemologies

In Western epistemology, people ask: How can we know? But in the Vedic epistemology, we can ask a more fundamental question: Can we know? The possibility of knowledge is assumed in Western epistemology. But because the world is an illusion in Vedic philosophy, almost everyone is ignorant by default. Knowledge can be obtained only by giving up the cheating propensity. Thus, everyone will not know because they will not give up their cheating.

A theory of knowledge can never be a universal "scientific method" adopted by everyone to know everything at all places and times without changing a person's attitude. A scientific method that disregards or separates the knower's attitudes from the knowing process can never lead to the truth, because it discounts the very reason that a person is in a certain type of world at a place and time. The method of knowing is deeply personal and not objective.

Thus, there is no answer to "How can we know?" because there is no answer to the problem of hallucination, misperception, misinterpretation, and cheating. Even if we meet a teacher, we don't know if he is not a cheater. Even if we see him, you don't know if this is not merely our hallucination. Even if we hear him speaking, you don't know if we are not misperceiving the sounds of his speech. Even if he speaks simply, we don't know if we are misinterpreting what he is saying. Every "solution" to the four problems of epistemology suffers from one or more of the same four problems. Hence, there is no objective answer to the problem of knowing.

The subjective answer to the problems of epistemology is that we have to give up the cheating propensity. If we remove cheating, then other forms of māyā—hallucination, misperception, and misinterpretation—automatically disappear. Therefore, near exclusive focus in the Vedic system is no removing cheating, because that naturally removes māyā. When our cheating is removed, then we get a true teacher. Otherwise, we only get cheaters. When our cheating is removed, then the problems of hallucination, misperception, and misinterpretation are also resolved through careful hearing from the teacher, while shunning or avoiding all cheaters.

The True Cure of the Material Illusion

The first step in knowledge is *morality*. We do not begin with microscopes and telescopes because they too are suffering from the four human defects. We do not try to create more or better mathematics because these are suffering from the four human defects. We always begin with character development because this is the only way to know the truth.

The degrees and certificates accumulated by a person do not make him a teacher. We can go to the best colleges, get the most advanced degrees, and yet not know anything because the criterion for knowing is the removal of the four human defects. A school that doesn't impart moral education as the most essential foundation of knowledge imparts ignorance.

The modern education system deemphasizes morality, which is considered the entry gate into knowledge in Vedic epistemology. Students going to schools and colleges are involved in illicit sexual affairs, intoxication, meat eating, and deceiving. The teachers imparting education in such schools and colleges are often involved in the same types of immoralities, if not much worse. Their criteria for graduation is passing examinations by cramming books without character development. Hence, the education system can never produce knowledge.

Religions and the Problem of Morality

Thus, the fundamental difference between a Brahmana and an academic is morality. Both can read books. Both can learn languages. But the Brahmana knows due to the cultivation of morality while the academic is ignorant due to neglect of morality. The Vedic system rejects the opinions of those who haven't undergone moral development, which means giving up the cheating propensity. It can take many forms, such as (a) making sacrifices for others, (b) showing kindness toward others, (c) never lying, and (d) presenting the truth in the least ambiguous manner. If these principles are practiced in life, then māyā stops deluding us.

Religions are not immune to cheating. If a religion tries to maximize the taking and minimize the giving, then it is rooted in cheating. Thereby, all religions are not divine. Some are also the byproducts of delusion. Material energy produces delusional sciences and religions. In a delusional science, a false conception of the world is presented. In a delusional religion, a false conception of the self is presented. Generally, a false conception of the world emerges from a false conception of the self. Therefore, if some science has followed some religion that provided a false conception of the self, then the science that follows it will always be false.

Thus, purifying the conception of the self through a moral life of kindness, cleanliness, austerity, and truthfulness is the preliminary and fundamental criterion to know the truth. We have to remove the cheating from a person's heart before hallucinations, misperceptions, and misinterpretations will be removed. The removal of the cheating propensity is each person's prerogative. The subsequent removal of hallucination, misperception, and misinterpretation is automatically the effect of the removal of adverse effects on a person by nature.

All epistemological problems begin with entry into māyā, which happens due to cheating, so the process can only be reversed by removing the cheating. A teacher can tell us that the world is meaningful and purposeful and by disregarding that meaning and purpose we are in delusion. But the teacher cannot cleanse a person's heart of the cheating propensity. That every student has to do himself. Since very few do it, therefore, very few are knowledgeable.

The Less Known Problematic Origins of Calculus

The Origin of Calculus in Change vs. Constant

Underlying every kind of scientific theory is a fundamental conundrum between change and constant. For example, if we want to do sociology, we must talk about how society is changing. But in so talking, we have to say that there is a thing called "society", which changes in some ways but remains the same society. The new and old societies are the same in one sense and different in another. But how can we make those two claims without a contradiction? Similarly, while doing economics, we have to talk about how an economy is changing. But in so talking, we have to say that there is a thing called "economy" which changes in some ways but remains the same economy. The new and old economies are the same in one sense and different in another. But how can we make those two contradictory claims without a contradiction?

This problem occupied early Greek philosophers—Heraclitus and Parmenides—and had a paralyzing effect on scientific thinking for 2000 years, to a point that no scientific theory could be developed until the logical contradiction between change and constant had been resolved.

When Newton created modern science, he found a solution to this problem based on methods that Indian mathematicians were using to compute planetary trajectories. These methods were employed to compute ritual timings. They came to be known as calculus. This solution has had an enduring effect since Newton and is used in all areas of modern science because no other solution to the change vs. constant problem has been proposed or found since then.

Calculus, however, is a deeply flawed solution to the change vs. constant problem, and I will discuss the flaws in calculus along with the correct solution to the same problem. We will trace the origins of this problem in Greek philosophy, why these problems had made science impossible, how calculus was created, and despite its numerous successes, why it has become a dead end for science today, before talking about the correct solution.

Change vs. Constant in Western Philosophy

The problem begins with the debates between Parmenides and Heraclitus sometime around 500 BCE. Heraclitus claimed that change is the only constant and there is no such thing as "being" as he likened everything to a flowing river. To say that I went for a bath in the Ganga is meaningless for him because "you can never step in the same river twice". Ganga is also a meaningless word for Heraclitus because it assumes the existence of the same thing day after day, when it is just flowing water. By extension, there is no such thing as an economy or a society that changes because reality is only change and flux.

This argument is so good that Parmenides had to counterclaim that change is impossible and that a flowing river is an illusion. There is only one thing called "being", Parmenides claimed, and for any change to occur, a "being" must cease to exist and become a non-being, followed by the appearance of another being that was previously non-being. Change, therefore, involves a logical contradiction in a being becoming non-being and followed by a non-being becoming a being. Parmenides spent considerable effort in proving that being cannot become non-being and non-being cannot become being.

Change vs. Constant in Vedic Philosophy

There is an easy solution to this problem, which Kṛṣṇa calls *dehina* and *deha*, and which we loosely call soul and body at present. The solution says that there are many potential states of the soul called bodies, and the soul goes from one state to another, or from body to body. Therefore, the bodies are changing while the soul is constant. The soul and the body are not the same, and yet both exist. Therefore, both change and constant exist simultaneously, and yet, they pertain to body and soul, respectively.

How the soul goes from one body to another is a complex process, but we can simplify it to "choice" for the moment. This simplification is not always true because time forces many changes in the body and this forced movement from body to body—often against the soul's choices—is called the soul's bondage in the world. The forced change causes the soul to change bodies from childhood to youth to old bodies in one life, and then to another childhood body in the next life. The distinction between the effects of time and the soul's choices is not important for the present discussion, so we can talk about "choice" as a generic solution to the succession of bodies that can be made either by the soul or by time.

Change vs. Constant in Judeo-Christianity

Greek philosophers did not have the above soul-body solution. Even if some Greeks believed in the soul, it never entered their philosophical speculations, and certainly never played a role in solving philosophical problems. Religion and philosophy had already been separated as faith vs. reason in Greek thinking. Hence, they had no answer to the change vs. constant problem. Their solution was to either deny change or constant.

While a soul-body distinction exists in Judeo-Christianity, we can never say that "I *am* a soul, and I *have* a body". Instead, we must say "I *am* the body, and I *have* a soul". For instance, people would commonly say: "May God have mercy upon your soul" rather than "May God have mercy upon you". This term was later adopted in legal discourse and is presently used by judges while pronouncing a death sentence.

In Judeo-Christianity, the soul is just like a coin in someone's pocket. The body moves, and the coin goes along with it. The pocket has the coin. The coin does not have a pocket. Thus, despite a soul-body distinction, Judeo-Christianity could not solve the change vs. constant problem, as it treated the soul as a property of the body rather than the body a property of the soul. The change vs. constant problem applies to the body.

Space vs. Time vs. Matter Distinction

An even more serious issue in Greek philosophy was the absence of the distinction between space, time, and matter. As we know, the Greeks had four elements, called Earth, Water, Fire, and Air, but not Ether, as in Vedic texts. So, people were walking on earth and through air, but never in space. Past, present, and future were illusions for Parmenides because there was only "being" which could never become another being. The concept of empty space—something devoid of Air, Water, Fire, and Earth—did not exist. Thus, neither time nor space existed for Parmenides. It was only material substance. Since change was denied, therefore, both time and space were unnecessary constructs, artifacts of the illusion of change.

Likewise, for Heraclitus, space was either Air or Fire, and a portion of that Air or Fire became Earth and Water. Since everything was simply flux, therefore, change and time were innate properties of the material substances, not separate from them. Time would be separate from material substance if there was an unchanging substance. Since everything was flux, therefore, time was also substance. Thus, we could not talk about motion *in* space and time. The space, time, and matter distinction was absent.

Cartesian Substance vs. Space and Time

Even when Descartes published Meditations in 1641, he called the body *res extensa* or "extended substance". He removed the four Greek elements of Earth, Water, Fire, and Air, and replaced them with one substance that had extension. He often equated *res extensa* to a "corporeal substance" meaning that which comprises the body. Descartes rejected the distinction between substance and form, which means that there is no Platonic world of forms with an ideal form of a cube or sphere which is embedded in a corporeal substance to create a corporeal cube or sphere. There was just a corporeal substance.

The "space" between two people was not empty space. It was also an extended substance, like the Air of Greeks. Since Cartesian ontology only includes two substances—*res extensa* and *res cogitans*—therefore, time had no independent existence. He sometimes called time a "mode of thought" and at other times he spoke about the "duration of existence", treating time as an attribute of the two substances. Thereby, the corporeal substance was the real thing and extension and duration were the substance's properties. Effectively, substance was not *in* space and time. Rather, space and time were *in* the substance.

When we put space and time in the substance, then we cannot solve the change vs. constant problem because the substance—like the society and economy—is both change and constant. If it changes, then it is longer constant. But if it remains constant, then it can no longer change. By adding space and time attributes to the corporeal substance, Cartesian metaphysics could be alternatively interpreted either as Heraclitan becoming without a being or Parmenidean being without a becoming, but never both.

Serendipitous Newtonian Solutions

Thus, even until the time of Descartes, there was no resolution to the problem of change vs. constant created in Greek times, and the distinction between space, time, and matter did not exist. The resolution to both these problems appears for the first time in Newton's writing published as Principia in 1687—46 years after Cartesian Meditations. In Principia, Newton provided a solution to the Greek problem of change vs. constant, while separating space, time, and matter to create a theory of motion.

It is rather astounding that such innovation in thinking happens all of a sudden and out of the blue. But it is not so amazing if we understand that Newtonian innovations were not truly his. He was taking them from Freemasonry texts, which had all these concepts. Newton indirectly acknowledged Freemasons for these ideas by saying: "If I have seen further than others, it is by standing upon the shoulders of giants." The "others" in this case were Descartes, Copernicus, Galileo, Kepler, and such. The "giants" in this case were Freemasons who remain unnamed and unquoted for reasons that we can only guess today.

Masonry had been persecuted for centuries prior by the Catholic Church. It had been given acceptance in Europe after the

Protestant Reformation about a century prior to Newton. Those who were earlier called Masons were now calling themselves Freemasons (since they were free from persecution). But to attribute scientific breakthroughs to an erstwhile persecuted minority would be highly embarrassing to Christianity. Not crediting them would be problematic in case the connection was later discovered. So, and this is my guess, Newton chose to attribute breakthroughs to "giants" without naming them.

Narratives on the Origins of Calculus

At this juncture, I will like to take a detour into how the story of the invention of calculus is presently told. Here are some pertinent quotes from the Wikipedia article on the History of Calculus:

- Egypt: The ancient period introduced some of the ideas that led to integral calculus, but does not seem to have developed these ideas in a rigorous and systematic way. Calculations of volumes and areas, one goal of integral calculus, can be found in the Egyptian Moscow papyrus (c. 1820 BC), but the formulas are only given for concrete numbers, some are only approximately true, and they are not derived by deductive reasoning.
- India: Some ideas on calculus later appeared in Indian mathematics, at the Kerala school of astronomy and mathematics. Madhava of Sangamagrama in the 14th century, and later mathematicians of the Kerala school, stated components of calculus such as the Taylor series and infinite series approximations. However, they did not combine many differing ideas under the two unifying themes of the derivative and the integral, show the connection between the two, and turn calculus into the powerful problem-solving tool we have today.
- Greeks: Eudoxus used the method of exhaustion, which foreshadows the concept of the limit, to calculate areas and volumes, while Archimedes developed this idea further, inventing heuristics which resemble the methods of

> integral calculus. Greek mathematicians are also credited with a significant use of infinitesimals. Democritus is the first person recorded to consider seriously the division of objects into an infinite number of cross-sections, but his inability to rationalize discrete cross-sections with a cone's smooth slope prevented him from accepting the idea. At approximately the same time, Zeno of Elea discredited infinitesimals further by his articulation of the paradoxes which they seemingly create.

Egyptians and Indians who had formulas and numbers did not "develop them in a rigorous and systematic way", "did not derive them by deductive reasoning" and could not "turn calculus into the powerful problem-solving tool we have today". Meanwhile, Greeks paralyzed by their controversies about being and becoming were "prevented from accepting their own ideas" by "paradoxes that infinitesimals seemingly create". Never mind the fact that Newton would have named the "giants" if they were Greeks. Never mind the basic problem of change vs. constant and the paralyzing effects that Parmenides and Heraclitus had. There is something to be learned from this, namely, that history is easily distorted by interpreting facts using a biased lens that unduly favors one side over the other.

Paradoxes Created by Zeno of Elea

While we are on this topic, we should talk about the problem of infinitesimals created by Zeno, a disciple and supporter of Parmenides, and hence, a proponent of the impossibility of motion. He created several paradoxes of motion to justify the Parmenidean position in which a changing world is an illusion because there is just a being, which cannot become non-being, on the path to becoming another being.

The simplest of these paradoxes says: Achilles is in a race with a tortoise, with the tortoise having a head start of 100 meters. When Achilles has run 100 meters, the tortoise has gone a little further by 2 meters. When Achilles has run 2 meters, the tortoise has gone a little further by a few centimeters. Thus, Achilles is always behind the tortoise. Hence, the quickest runner can never overtake the slowest runner.

Another paradox says: An arrow cannot move to a place that it is presently not situated, in infinitesimal time, because no time elapses for the arrow to move to that place. Similarly, the arrow cannot move to the place where it is already situated at present because it is already there. Thereby, the arrow is always motionless. Even if the arrow has been released from a bow, it can never reach its target destination.

If we look carefully, the Achilles Paradox divides space into infinitesimals and the Arrow Paradox divides time into infinitesimals and concludes Achilles can never overtake the tortoise and the arrow can never hit its target. Of course, we see Achilles overtaking the tortoise and the arrow hitting its target. However, if these were real, then we would never see those things. Since we see them, they must be illusions.

Later Developments in Western Thinking

The philosophies of Parmenides and Heraclitus are what we call māyāvāda and śūnyavāda in the Vedic tradition. According to māyāvāda, there is a being called Brahman, but all becoming—seen as a world—is an illusion. According to śūnyavāda, there is just becoming without any being, and hence there is no Brahman, and even as māyā may be perceived, it has no reality, hence ultimately nothing exists. Both māyāvāda and śūnyavāda are antiscientific philosophies due to their antirealist attitudes. This is why Buddhists (who follow śūnyavāda) and Advaitins (who follow māyāvāda) never made any scientific discoveries. They only reject the sense of meaning and purpose in the present world and life.

Greeks were rescued from this sense of meaningless and purposeless existence by Plato, when he talked about form-substance dualism, with a transcendent world of pure forms that made the present world of substance meaningful and purposeful because the transcendent forms were partially and imperfectly reflected in the world. Platonism could never be justified because no forms could ever be defined. Greeks just anointed themselves as pure humans and treated other races as imperfect humans at best.

Aristotle then junked the imaginary Platonic transcendentalism by separating forms into "theoretical" and "practical" categories with the former being public rationality and the latter being private belief. Even the separation of private and public was junked by the Romans as the Bible came to be regarded as the only source of truth, which had to be accepted on faith and could not be analyzed rationally.

To ignore this historical trajectory and say that the Greeks were close to discovering calculus is quite facetious. To disregard the fact that Newton did not attribute a single Greek for his discovery, and instead recognized unnamed giants, means that the Greeks were hindering and not assisting progress. To disregard the effects of problems created by Zeno's Paradoxes, which are widely discussed even today, is to ignore what they entail. By disregarding all these problems, we can never understand the significance that calculus presently assigns to the concepts of continuity and smoothness of trajectories. Therefore, the story of calculus as is commonly told today is designed to obscure the truth rather than reveal it.

The Theory of the Soul in Vedic Texts

Before we move further, I would like to talk about the tripartite nature of the soul in Vedic texts and how this tripartite description is absolutely crucial to the solution to the problem of change and constant. The three aspects of the soul are called sat-chit-ānanda, and for the sake of our present conversation, we can call them thinking-thought-thinker. The thinker produces a will. The will acts on a repository of ideas to pick an idea. After the idea has been selected, consciousness attaches to it to think it. But if this vocabulary seems difficult, then we can also use three words—will, idea, and awareness. There is a repository of ideas from which an idea is selected by will and then awareness attaches to the idea to know it.

The will or choice is discrete. The thought picked by that will or choice is also discrete. Since awareness moves from one thought to another, therefore, even the knowing of the idea is discrete. However, even when there is no thought, there is still self-awareness which we call "I". This "I" produces a will, which then selects a thought, and attaches to that thought to become aware of it. We can call this process "I am X", where "I" is the thinker, "X" is the thought, and "am" is the thinking. "I am X" is thinker thinking thought. The "I" is continuous, but the will, thought selection, and awareness of thought are discrete.

As the thinker goes through a succession of thoughts, the being becomes thoughts without going through non-being. Likewise, the continuous succession of thoughts—which we can call becoming—are not the denial of a being. The discreteness of successive thoughts is not the denial of the continuity of the thinker. The continuity of the thinker is not the rejection of the discreteness of thoughts. Thus, being is not contrary to becoming and continuity is not contrary to discreteness. Due to the discreteness of thoughts, the concept of infinitesimals created by Zeno is false. The thinker doesn't get fractional thoughts. He is either thinking or not thinking. Each thought is finite and not infinitely small. The thinker jumps through thoughts one after another without creating any discontinuity in his existence.

Thus, all problems of being vs. becoming are resolved if we use the thinker-thinking-thought model of change. Likewise, the problem of infinitesimals created by Zeno ceases to exist in this model of change. Any potential contradiction between discreteness and continuity also ceases to exist likewise. The being is continuous and the becoming is discrete. The "I" is the constant and the "am X" is the change. By going through a succession of "I am X", there is an unchanging "I" and a changing "am X" attribute.

Science From the Theory of the Soul

This solution to the problem of being vs. becoming, constant vs. change, and continuous vs. discrete is applied to everything in Vedic philosophy. For instance, society and economy are also some "I". When the society or economy evolves, the same "I" gets a new "am X" attribute. Thereby, we can say that the same society and economy have changed to a new state. Similarly, there is an "I" called Ganga which then goes through successive stages called the "flowing water". When we step into flowing water day after day, we are stepping into the same river called Ganga, even though the flowing water is different.

The person who enters a society or an economy has entered the awareness of some "I". The person who steps into the flowing water of Ganga has entered the awareness of Ganga. When they step out of Ganga, they have left the awareness of Ganga. If they leave a society or economy, they have stepped out of the awareness of the "I" that identified that society or economy as a unique being or individual.

The Cartesian body is not a "corporeal substance". It is thought. The Cartesian mind is also not a non-material substance. It is an "I". The connection between mind and body is not mysterious. It is simply the connection between some "I" and some "X" to produce "I am X". Since the "X" can be changed without destroying the "I", therefore, there can be a succession of bodies of the soul. Even if the soul goes to sleep and then wakes up, still there is a succession of bodies from "I am X" to "I am Y" which follows the same process as the numerous X's that the I had previously attached to as its personal attributes. There is strict ordering between I and X, such that "I am X" is correct but "X is I" is incorrect. This means that the soul has a body, but the body doesn't have a soul, nor are the body and soul identical in any sense. The soul and body become identical if and only if there is an "X" that the "I" can be eternally attached to. Hence, the difference between an eternal and a temporary body is that "I am X" can be eternal or temporary.

Therefore, if we want to do any kind of science—let it be economics, biology, sociology, cosmology, or physics—the paradigm is always the evolution of "I" through a succession of "X". Each such paradigm is identical to that of a fixed *dehina* and a changing *deha*. If we know how the soul changes bodies, then it applies to how the Ganga flows, how an economy goes up or down, how a society rises or falls, and how an object moves. There is only one subject—namely, the science of how the soul goes from body to body—because there is one resolution to the problem of constant vs. change, continuous vs. discrete, and being vs. becoming. Another resolution to this problem is not needed if this resolution always works. We only have to prove that this resolution to the problem of being vs. becoming always works.

The Essence of the Newtonian Solution

Newtonian calculus eschewed all these principles found in the Vedic texts and envisioned an alternative idea of change and constant in which a particle moves through infinitesimal locations in space and time. The particle is the being and its successive positions in space and time are becoming. This requires separating space, time, and matter (matter is now a particle moving through space and time). Through this separation, Newton got rid of all the historical problems created by Heraclitus, Parmenides, Zeno, and Descartes. The world is now not a Cartesian *res extensa*. It is actually two such extensa—space and time—with the particle moving through the extensa in infinitesimal steps. There is no problem of being becoming non-being during change because that non-being is space and time whereas the being is the particle; the same thing is not both being and non-being, so the contradiction doesn't exist. Since there is indeed a being—the particle—therefore, the world is not simply flux as was the case for Heraclitus.

All problems could be solved by solving Zeno's Paradoxes—e.g., the Achilles and Arrow Paradoxes. The answer required saying that infinitesimal is not actually zero, but something that *tends to zero*. We can make the infinitesimal as small as we like, but it will never be precisely zero because if it were precisely zero, then the Arrow would never move forward and Achilles can never overtake the tortoise.

The innovation of calculus is redefining the infinitesimal as neither finite nor zero. To quote Wikipedia again: *An infinitesimal number is a quantity that is closer to zero than any standard real number, but that is not zero. The word infinitesimal comes from a 17th-century Modern Latin coinage infinitesimus, which originally referred to the "infinity-th" item in a sequence.* An infinitesimal exists in the no-man's land between 0 and the smallest conceivable number, and it originates in infinite convergent series.

Indian Origins of the Newtonian Solution

Infinite convergent series were invented in India to calculate values of real numbers to arbitrarily desirable levels of accuracy. For instance, the number ϖ can be defined to the accuracy of ten decimal places as 3.1415926535. We don't always need so much accuracy. Most school and college students just equate ϖ to 3.14. But if we were doing a satellite launch, we better use a more accurate value.

Clearly, we cannot obtain more precise values of ϖ by drawing a circle on paper because every scale we use has a limit in the smallest granularity it can measure. To measure the precise value of a planet or star in the sky, the canvas on which we draw the circle must be far bigger than the earth. Accurate astronomy is hence not possible unless we define ϖ to increasing levels of accuracy. Infinite convergent series were invented in India for precisely the purpose to define numbers like ϖ to an arbitrary desired accuracy. The infinite series for ϖ for instance is $1 - 1/3 + 1/5 - 1/7 + 1/9 - \ldots = \varpi/4$. It takes lots of steps to get to accurate values, but each step is very easy, and we can truncate the steps whenever we want to get a less precise value that suffices our needs. We need a few decimal places to get the circumference of a dome and more decimal places to compute the precise points of celestial planetary conjunctions.

This is then the origin of infinitesimals—the infinity-th item in a series of numbers that progressively converges to a *limit value*—in this case, ϖ. Of course, we don't have to go to infinity. We can truncate it after an arbitrarily chosen—although sufficiently large—number of steps. The incremental additions become smaller and smaller, which is why the infinitesimal can get smaller without ever being 0.

We have to remember that this is just a calculation tool and not reality. We cannot chop off some steps in reality and expect the planets to complete their revolutions in time. By chopping off those steps, the planets would start lagging behind. Knowing everything to infinite precision requires infinite steps and hence infinite time. Therefore, truncating a convergent series can never be called reality. These were meant only to calculate the precise time for a ritual—sometimes called a muhurta—because a ritual that begins and ends within the muhurta gives better results. To know the time by which the ritual can begin and the time by which it must end, mathematics was necessary.

How Indian Mathematics Benefitted Newton

The mathematics that Indians had invented for doing rituals was useful for architecture too, especially if you had to build an architecture aligned with specific cosmic events, such as a temple precisely facing the sun when the sun enters a particular star sign. The same methods of calculation that were used for calculating the precise muhurta for a ritual were useful for calculating the precise orientation of temples. This is how masonry got involved in mathematics, and this knowledge traveled to other parts of the world through masons, although the inventors of that mathematics were ritualistic Brahmanas.

The fact that Brahmanas were doing muhurta calculations for rituals doesn't mean that this had anything to do with the science of rituals itself. Rituals involved mantra pronunciation, a mantra had a meaning, and reality was modeled as meaning. Mathematics instead does geometric computations without any semantics. The fact that the Brahmana would do both the muhurta calculation and the ritual at the appointed time, leads to the modern confusion that mathematics is actually the Brahmanical science when mathematics was simply a tool while real science was the chanting of mantras. The mantra science needed a lot of philosophy of linguistics and meaning while mathematics needed approximations.

Newton got formulas for infinite convergent series through masons and realized that the answers to the problems raised by Zeno's paradoxes lay in saying that an Arrow or Achilles moves an infinitesimal step forward in an infinitesimal time, neither of which is precisely 0. An infinitesimal has a small *length*, but zero does not. That makes all the difference because Zeno's Paradoxes depend on zero-length points in space and time. If these are not zero, and yet, arbitrarily small, then Zeno's Paradoxes don't exist.

For this solution to actually work, we also need to separate space, time, and matter, which already existed in the Indian calculations of muhurta where a planetary body is moving in space and time, so the world is not a plenum or substance, as was the case up until the time of Descartes. Instead, that substance was replaced by three distinct concepts of space, time, and matter, with precise models of calculating the motion of bodies to predict the specific time at which they arrive at a specific place.

How Newton Depended on Observations

Newton only needed to replace the angular speed of planetary movements used in such calculations (which had been determined over ages through empirical observation) with a causal explanation of that angular speed (i.e., the angle by which the planet moves in unit time). This work had already been done by Johannes Kepler where he showed—based on the Copernican hypothesis of a heliocentric solar system—that the angular speed of a planet is inversely proportional to its distance from the sun.

Newton's ingenuity lay in postulating a "gravitational force" pulling the planets toward the sun to explain the angular speeds that Kepler had observed. He was assisted in this solution by children tying stones to a string and rotating them around—(a) the planet was the stone, (b) the gravitational force was the string tugging at the stone, (c) the planetary angular speed was how fast the stone was rotating. Newton had to make a formula that will reduce the angular speed of rotation with the increasing length of the rope and it turned out to be an inverse squared law. Everything else was casting that formula in an ordinary language by either inventing new names or applying familiar ones to symbols in the formula.

The fact is that one could *predict* planetary positions based on Kepler's measurements. There would be no *explanation* of planetary movement, but it would work. It would not be precise without the infinite convergent series formulae, but it would work. It would be just a hallucination without a solution to Zeno's paradoxes, but it would work. It could be a planet stepping into the sky-river, but it would work. Three out of the four problems—hallucination, river in the sky, and imprecise prediction—were solved by the postulate of infinitesimals. The fourth problem of explaining the motion based on gravity was Newton's invention, although he had help in this solution from children playing with ropes and stones. The story of the apple falling on Newton's head is either pure fiction or at best an unrelated fact.

Problems of Continuity and Smoothness

Infinitesimals allow us to write quantities like $\partial x/\partial t$ because they are arbitrarily small and yet not 0. But they also force restrictions on the possible trajectories. The trajectory cannot be discrete and unsmooth because then ∂x would be finite and ∂t would be 0, and the result would be $\partial x/\partial t = \infty$. These restrictions do not exist when we talk about a thinker thinking thought. A thinker may think logically progressing thoughts, and his mind may then be said to move continuously and smoothly. However, a thinker can also be distracted from one thought to another and his mind would be discontinuous and unsmooth. The thinker thinking thought doesn't mandate continuity and smoothness, whereas calculus does.

If you take a pencil and try to draw a line on paper, the question is: What is the next point in the line? Should the pencil move upward or downward? Should it go backward or forward? Should it jump or move smoothly? These are choices. But calculus eliminates them. The pencil cannot jump, and it should not take a discrete left or right, up or down, or forward or backward turn. Even if the pencil turns, it should do it slowly and smoothly. Thus, the hand should never draw a triangle or square because these have sharp vertices. A sharp vertex in calculus means that that rate of change denoted by $\partial x/\partial t = \infty$. If we get one infinity in a series, the sum will also be infinite. To eliminate sharp vertices, the hand should never draw a triangle or a square. Circles, ellipses, and straight or curved lines are fine because they don't have sharp vertices. Thereby, the use of infinitesimals puts a constraint on the hand holding the pencil.

The constraint on the hand is called *determinism*. It is created by assuming that the hand cannot move the pencil in all the ways that the hand is capable of moving. By constraining the hand, determinism is created and choice is destroyed. Of course, if choice exists, then calculus will be proven inadequate. The hand may sometimes change position and direction discretely, which then breaks calculus. Since calculus is the foundation of everything in modern science, hence, discretizing hand motion breaks science. This is why science is indeterministic—the hand can jump up or down, left or right, forward or backward, discretely. So, if we assume calculus, it may work for some hand movements—where the hand is drawing circles and ellipses. But it will fail for other cases—when the hand draws triangles and squares.

The solution to this problem requires rejecting calculus as a model of reality. It may be used for those changes that are like circles and ellipses, although even then it is not the nature of reality. Calculus certainly breaks when the change is like a square or triangle. After throwing calculus in the dustbin of history, we can return back to Zeno's Paradoxes and solve them with the thinker thinking thought model, which accommodates both discrete and continuous, being and becoming, constant and change.

The Problem of Choice and Indeterminism

Newton's mechanics is not deterministic. If two cars crash into each other, we cannot use Newtonian equations to predict the outcome. We can only use Newton's mechanics while they are running on the road. Even if determinism is observed, such as in the case of billiard ball collisions, the explanation is not deterministic because when two particles collide, they can recoil in many directions since the colliding particle is dimensionless in theory, so every direction is equally good. This indeterminism is not seen in billiard ball collisions due to the finite size of the ball, which makes all directions non-equivalent.

Thereby, even when the phenomena are deterministic, the theory is indeterministic. Otherwise, if the balls collide and disintegrate into many pieces, then the phenomenon is also not deterministic. The problem of indeterminism in Newton's theories is not realized by limiting its application to (a) finite-sized balls, and (b) that do not disintegrate on collision. If we merely accept that all balls are finite-sized, then the calculus based on infinitesimals would be destroyed. If we merely accept that some balls disintegrate on a collision, then the calculus based on continuity and smoothness will be destroyed. Hence, to preserve calculus we have to pretend that all changes, in reality, are infinitesimal, continuous, and smooth.

These assumptions then create the illusion of determinism and are used by many ignorant scientists and philosophers as a counter to free will. They don't know that calculus is preventing the hand from drawing a square and triangle and permitting the hand to draw a circle and ellipse. Nature is not preventing the hand from drawing a square or triangle; calculus is. Therefore, calculus is not a model of reality. It is incapable of predicting and explaining all discontinuous and unsmooth phenomena—which are, by the way—the only phenomena due to atomic theory. This, as we have discussed, is because all choices are discrete. Sometimes that discreteness can be approximately modeled as smoothness and continuity. But that is largely an exception. The rule is that everything is discrete due to the quantization of reality.

The Problem of Quantization of Reality

Quantization breaks the assumption of infinitesimals, which breaks calculus, which returns us to Zeno's Paradoxes. Quantization has taken us back to Greek times when Parmenides and Heraclitus were arguing about being vs. becoming. 2500 years have passed, but we are back to where we started—in terms of understanding the nature of reality, finding correct models for reality, and building truthful theories. In some ways, we may even be worse off than the time in 500 BCE, when most of nature was pristine, millions of additional life forms existed, and the fear of the planet killing most people did not exist, although people were still killing each other.

Indeterminism is the law of unintended consequences. We don't expect something to happen, but it happens. But we cannot simply blame the problem on a "law" when we chose the "law" called calculus which then leads us to the "law" of unintended consequences. We have to give up both kinds of laws.

Whatever people call the problem of "quantum gravity" is actually a problem about the quantization of space and time because gravity has been reduced to the properties—such as curvature—of space and time. To unify the theory of space and time with the theory of matter and energy, we have to quantize everything. We cannot have discrete particles of matter and energy floating in a continuous space and time. But we cannot quantize space and time because it will break the infinitesimals used as $\partial x/\partial t$.

The fact is that quantization will make some locations bigger and some locations smaller. Quantization will make some moments longer and some moments shorter. How will we know what is bigger or smaller when the scale used to measure big and small is itself becoming bigger and smaller? The answer is simple—we have to use something that doesn't become bigger or smaller due to changes in locations and times. That *constant* thing is the soul. It can experience longer and shorter moments. It can know what is bigger and smaller because it is itself not changed by changing locations and times.

The Problem of Relativization of Reality

The problem of relativity is "I am X" where "X" is a temporary, changing, and momentary designation of the "I" similar to ordinary designations of the "I" as man and woman, black and white, husband and wife. When the "I" acquires a temporary "X", then it seems different from other "I" with a different "X". Then, if "I am X" interacts with some "I am Y", it gets a subjective deviant understanding of Y because its own designation is X, and it is unable to truly know the "I" thinking "I am Y". X and Y are called "coordinate reference frames" in the theory of relativity. But since X and Y keep changing (change is called motion and acceleration), therefore, every "I" with "X" and "Y" misjudges each other to preclude knowledge.

The misjudgment is called "length contraction" and "time dilation" in the theory of relativity. This means that each observer, due to its own conditioning by X and Y, selects and rejects certain aspects of each other, while neglecting the other aspects. This is similar to an observer looking at one side of the cube, and thinking that the other sides don't exist, or that there is just a flat surface and not a cube. Meanwhile, other observers are looking at other faces of the cube and calling the same thing a different face. The different observers cannot reconcile the different faces into a coherent understanding, and they cannot agree with the other observers.

This problem is called the elephant and the five blind men in Indian philosophy. Each blind man sees one aspect of the elephant, and claims that it is the full elephant, but cannot agree with others who describe the same thing differently. Relativization is the result of not being able to see the full truth because that full truth is not visible to everyone precisely due to their identification with some X, which then precludes the understanding of Y. When X and Y misunderstand Z, and each other, they enter into a conflict about whose version is true, like the blind men who argue with each other about what the elephant truly is.

Reconciling Quantization and Relativization

The above two problems can be resolved if a quantum is also an observer's perspective. For instance, we can treat the elephant's parts such as its leg, tail, stomach, ear, and trunk as quanta, each blind man as one perspective on the elephant which receives one quantum and claims that it is the whole truth, but they cannot reconcile all these quanta into the elephant. Reconciliation requires three other possibilities: (a) each blind man can alternately walk over the place of the other blind man and see what he is seeing, (b) he can become a visionary to see the whole elephant, and (c) he can further understand that the elephant is an "I" attached to some temporary "X" calling itself "I am X".

Through these processes, we can progressively dissolve the mutual exclusion of the various quanta and perspectives. If there is mutual exclusion, then there will be disagreement, competition, and unhappiness. If there is mutual inclusion, then there will be agreement, cooperation, and happiness. Thus, the Vedic texts talk about matter and spirit as duality (exclusion) and non-duality (inclusion).

The fact is that the tail and trunk of an elephant are mutually defined although blind men cannot see that. They can just see that the tail and trunk cannot be varied independently; changing the tail also changes the trunk. This is quantum entanglement. But due to blindness, they cannot accept that the same thing is both tail and trunk, and yet, neither of them. Thus, the problem of quantization and relativization is the result of blindness. The problem doesn't exist for the visionary. Then, X and Y are not mutually exclusive or contradictory.

When science transitions us from disagreement, competition, and unhappiness to agreement, cooperation, and happiness, then it becomes the solution to the problems of life. This science is not the calculus of infinitesimals, based on motion and acceleration, relying on force and mass, and suffering from the dualities of change vs. constant, discrete vs. continuous, and being vs. becoming. This science is not imbued with indeterminism and the law of unintended consequences. It is not the victim of dualisms such as mind vs. body, religion vs. science, faith vs. reason, private vs. public, and subjective vs. objective.

The truth has always been available in Vedic texts. The practice and realization of that truth required some rituals, which required some mathematics, which went from Brahmanas to masons, traveled to various parts of the world, and eventually became calculus and gravitational theory. This history is obscured at present to preserve the prestige of those who don't want to acknowledge that they took something from somewhere which was never meant to be used in the way it was used, and this is a dead end now. Now we need a new philosophy even to solve the problems created by calculus. Until then, no fundamental discoveries will ever be made. We are now back to Zeno's Paradoxes, a 2500-year-old problem, and we should start thinking about the Parmenides-Heraclitus debate again.

Cultural Assumptions in European Science

The Problem of Simplicity and Complexity

All the fundamental differences between European science and the Vedic system can be traced back to an assumption about *simplicity* in European thinking. Factually, ordinary sense perception is immensely complex. Food, for instance, has taste, smell, color, taste, texture, shape, weight, hardness, and so on. Clothing, housing, families, societies, flora, and fauna are also immensely complex. Moreover, no two things in the world are identical. No two people, apples, oranges, deers, or societies are identical. When we put two things into the same class, we ignore their differences, such as when we call two things "apples".

The assumption that reality is simple can be traced back to Greek times in the formulation called *universalism* under which concepts such as an "apple" are the true nature of things when they are merely an approximation. The term "apple" simply tells us that it is not an orange, banana, or grape. It does not say that two things in the "apple" class are identical. Classes are methods of identifying *similarities* between things rather than their *identity*. Any system of knowledge that equates similarity to identity runs the risk of oversimplification.

These problems were faced in Greek times in the attempt to define ordinary concepts such as "man". A man who has lost one leg in a war is still called a man although we cannot equate this designation to identity with other men. At best, these are similarities. Greeks solved this problem by talking about an *ideal man*, that exists in a Platonic world of pure forms. Everyone else in this world then became a *non-ideal* man. The result of this postulate was that in the other world, all men must look, behave, think, and feel identically. Whatever seemed to deviate from a pre-defined norm of ideality became non-ideal, evil, devilish, and so forth.

When applied to ordinary things, such as food and clothing, it means that there must be good and evil foods and clothes. Since there can only be one ideal food, therefore, everyone who eats just that one thing is good but everyone else who eats other things is evil. All who wear one type of clothes must be good and everyone else who wears other clothes are evil. Thus simplification became *universalism* and the destruction of variety. Simplicity was forced on everyone by calling one thing ideal and everything else non-ideal, evil, devilish, and so forth.

Mathematical Origins of Simplicity

The Greek attitude toward simplification originates in geometry. There is a precise definition of words like circle, rectangle, and triangle. A triangular thing, with non-straight edges, is not truly a triangle. It is just a non-ideal triangle. A rectangular thing, with non-right-angle corners, is not truly a rectangle. It is just a non-ideal rectangle. A circular thing, which is not perfectly round, is not truly a circle. It is just a non-ideal circle. Thereby, truth in Greek thinking pertains to the ideal and falsity to the non-ideal. Aristotle called these ideality *theoretical forms* and truth was equated to precise alignment with an ideal form.

Problems with Greek attitudes then appeared in arithmetic. For instance, ideal numbers could only be whole numbers. A fractional number was non-ideal. Zero, which signified something absent or non-existent, could not be ideal because it did not exist. Negative numbers, which denoted less than nothing also could not be ideal. Pythagoras thought of the ideal world in terms of whole numbers, and Greeks could not develop a formal system of arithmetic because fractions, zero, and negative numbers were considered non-ideal, evil, devilish, etc.

Contrasting Attitudes in the Vedic System

The Vedic system also accepts ideality. But it is defined in terms of a *purpose* rather than an *idea*. Different kinds of foods serve different purposes. Spicy food serves to cure the ill-effects of cold and soothing food serves to cure the ill-effects of heat. We can wear light and airy clothes during summar and heavy and protective clothes during winter. Therefore, different foods and clothes are ideal for different situations because they serve the purpose better in different cases.

Truth now requires us to identify a Supreme Purpose. If life is lived to serve the Supreme Purpose, then different foods and clothes during summer and winter are both ideal. Variety is not evil, devilish, or non-ideal then. Conversely, the same variety becomes evil, devilish, or non-ideal when used inappropriately out of context. Nothing is good or evil per se because everything can be used in some situation and context. If there is a context in which something can be used permanently to serve the Supreme Purpose, then it is is ideal for that context.

In contrast to universalism, therefore, the Vedic system accommodates infinite variety as long as it is used in the most appropriate context. Rarely useful things are just rarely useful, not evil, devilish, or non-ideal. Often useful things are just common, not necessarily good and ideal. In a different time, place, or context, the same thing could become rarely useful.

Necessary Complexity in the Vedic System

When the Vedic system abandons universalism, and accommodates infinite variety, it also introduces a role for individuality and contextuality in addition to universality. My unique skills are my individual nature, useful in some contexts, useless in others, and harmful in yet others. As long as I use my skills in the useful (and not the useless and harmful) ways, I am ideal although I don't conform to a universal definition of man.

A word like "man" still denotes an ideal man, with abilities of an Original Man, called Manu. I am called a "man" due to the similarity with Manu and because I have descended from Manu. But

I cease to be an ideal man when I stop using my abilities in the ideal way that Manu will use them. At that juncture, I become a non-ideal, evil, or devilish man. I am still man in terms of my abilities. But I am no longer a man because I don't use my abilities appropriately.

This is how we get the necessity of non-binary logic, namely, that I am man in the sense of my abilities but not man in terms of using my abilities inappropriately. I could lose some of the abilities, such as a leg during a war, but continue to use the remaining abilities appropriately. I would then be not an ideal man in terms of abilities but still an ideal man in terms of using the remaining abilities most appropriately. Non-binary logic becomes essential when the same thing is a man and not man, or an ideal man and not ideal man.

Non-binary logics require *modalities*. I could be a man in one sense and not man in another sense, or an ideal man in one sense and not ideal man in another sense. These "senses" are the "modes". Ability and activity are two such modes, although there are infinite others. Binary logic always produces a contradiction when the same thing is called a man and not man. Modal logics do not do that. This is a virtue because it allows us to speak about a man with abilities using them inappropriately, or a man without abilities using them appropriately. This process is called *completeness*. Binary logic is always incomplete because contradictions are produced while speaking of capable men using their abilities inappropriately.

Complexity is Hard for the Universalist

Many people have complained that my writing is very complicated. They would like simplicity. Nearly all the people complaining about complexity have an ideological background in Western universalism. Nearly all the people reluctantly accepting this complexity are Indian, because even the Indian mind has been universalized due to the influence of impersonalism and European science. Someone wrote to me recently: "One reason I never get anywhere reading your books is that I feel like I either have to hold too much in my head at once to proceed with understanding, or

I need to ask for clarification right from the start and very often thereafter".

This problem is a natural result of oversimplification due to universalism, which postulates that reality must be reduced to fewer types of things, that the best situation of reality is that everything is just one type of thing. The Vedic system is just the opposite. There are infinite unique things with a common purpose. The uniqueness is individuality; the purpose is universality; and the use of uniqueness to fulfill the purpose in select times, places, and situation is contextuality. One thing could be X and not-X in different senses. This is necessary complexity. Anything less than this is incomplete in the desire to keep consistency.

East-West Cultural Contrasts

Complexity comes naturally to Indians and is very difficult for the West. I can cite some examples.

In Europe, for the longest time, the staple diet was meat and potatoes. Even bread was added very late in the diet. Until quite recently, the staple diet in America was meat, potatoes, bread, and peas or corn. There was only one spice—pepper. Contrast this to India. There are over 50 types of spices, over 10,000 dishes, and over 25 cuisines. Everything changes with the seasons. Each dish has 6 or 7 spices, and three or four ingredients, and is cooked in various stages such as frying followed by boiling, or boiling followed by frying. Everyone is used to immense variety and enjoys it in the same thing. Each cook makes the same dish differently. Each dish may have a different set of spices. Some spice was fried. Some spice was boiled. Some spice was roasted. The cuisine changes from place to place. The meal changes from season to season.

In Europe, for the longest time, there was only one dress. Shirts and pants for men and a blouse and skirt for women. Everything was in one color—mostly black or white. Contrast this to India. Before India's colonization, every woman had a unique collection of sarees. No two women had the same saree. That is because each saree was handwoven. Women would go to a weaver, and he had a big album of patterns, motifs, and colors. There were various types of threads based on mixing silk and cotton. Each woman would choose a unique set of threads, patterns, motifs, and colors and ask a weaver to weave a unique saree. Each woman was a unique customer. So how could she wear a common saree? If you mass-produced sarees in one design, nobody would buy them.

In Europe, religion means kneeling before God and repeating the same prayer every day. In India, there are hundreds of festivals and dozens of deities. Each deity has a unique mantra. Each deity eats a unique kind of food. There is a unique ritual for each deity.

I have been to the US at least a dozen times. Every time I spent about a month, sometimes 6 months. Every city looks more or less the same. Houses followed by malls followed by houses followed by malls. This is the result of universalism and simplification. In India, there is a car park on the first floor, a mall on the second floor, an office on the third floor, and homes on the fourth floor. It looks crazy, but it is also reality. We cannot reduce a building to one name or type of thing because it is many types of things at once.

Cultural Axioms Underlying Sciences

European science is built on the European lifestyle, namely, that reality is very *simple*. Everything is a particle. There are only two properties called position and momentum. And what doesn't fit into this European science is rejected as pseudo-science.

Vedic science is built on the Indian lifestyle, namely, that everything is very *complicated*. No two sarees are alike. No two dishes are alike. No two people are alike. No two deities are alike. No two festivals are alike. No two prayers are alike. No two seasons are alike.

Europeans started with the assumption that reality is simple. European science tries to simplify everything. Simplification is the scientific method in European science. Whenever you face complexity, you have to begin with simplifying assumptions. But Indians don't have that assumption. Reality is very complicated. We embrace this complexity. We enjoy this complexity. Then we try to understand and explain this complexity.

Therefore, while trying to understand the Vedic system, we have to begin with the problem in European science, namely, is reality so simple? We can study every subject and understand how much complexity exists and why no simple model works. When one simple model fails, then another simple model is created. In this way, we get thousands of models. No model can be reconciled with the other model. The attempt to attain simplicity results in immense complexity. Once we are convinced that the basic assumption of simplicity is false, then we can appreciate the Vedic system and understand complexity. If we don't know that simplicity doesn't work then we can never appreciate complexity. Our assumption has to be falsified by deep study.

Cultural Axioms Underlying Sciences

Ideas of simplicity and universalism in European thinking come from the Hellenistic and Mediterranean creation models in which the world is a combat between order and chaos. Order was masculine and chaos was feminine. The world was said to have been chaos in the beginning and then gods conquered the chaos and created order. The gods were good and the chaos was evil. To go to heaven, one had to conquer chaos and establish order. Order was equated to simplicity and chaos was equated to complexity.

We can contrast this to Indian thinking. Order is still masculine and chaos is still feminine. But chaos is a part of order and order is part of chaos. There is unity in diversity and there is diversity in unity. There is simplicity in complexity and there is complexity in simplicity. The masculine is inside the feminine and the feminine is inside the masculine.

The masculine and feminine are not in combat. They are playing with each other. The masculine doesn't conquer the feminine. He surrenders to the feminine. The feminine is the cook making thousands of dishes, dressed in unique beautiful sarees. The masculine sees this variety and says: I did not know that this was possible. But he enjoys it. The masculine is the enjoyer eating thousands of dishes admiring the versatility of the beautiful feminine making thousands of dishes dressed in gorgeous sarees.

The European mind simplifies reality. The Indian mind embraces complexity, understands it, and then explains it. The feminine is complexity and the masculine is simplicity. Everything is a combination of complexity and simplicity. Simplicity does not destroy complexity. They coexist and enjoy with each other happily.

Cultural Crimes of Universalism

European mentality of simplicity and universalism was responsible for the crimes of colonialism, the destruction of native cultures, and the denigration of ideologies far superior to Western thinking. Europeans considered monotheistic simplicity order and polytheistic complexity chaos. The order had to destroy chaos. The good had to kill the evil. The man was good and the woman was evil. Things are not very different at present.

But India doesn't consider women an evil. She is complexity and variety, the spices of life. The Vedic system is not monotheism because at the minimum there is a masculine and a feminine. Then that feminine is of immense complexity. The world she creates is also immensely complicated. Anyone trying to subdue this complexity with simplicity will run into a conflict with the woman, precisely reflecting the problem of describing complexity in terms of simplicity and running into incompleteness. Universalism has resulted in man-woman conflicts, because they are indeed opposite poles meant to dance together.

The Problems of Universalism

These problems are inescapable in Western thinking since the Hellenistic period. Christianity calls it monotheism. Enlightenment made it simple laws of nature. These are not true.

Therefore, we have to go back to the basics and ask: Is reality simple? Or, is it just a cultural assumption of Europeans? We can study each subject and discover its complexity. Then we study how different types of complexities are modeled by different sets of contradictory claims. When contradictory theories become the norm, then simplicity is refuted and replaced by immense complexity. Then we can never find unity in diversity because we began with the assumption that reality is simplicity.

Reality is not simple in the Vedic system. It is immensely complicated. But there is a unity in this variety. We don't understand unity by discarding variety. We embrace the complexity and then try to find the order in it.

The graphic at the top of the article shows how God is a geometer measuring reality with a protractor. This is a pictorial depiction of European science. Oversimplified, neglecting nuances and details, disregarding the variety, and reducing the universe to an angle and a length.

What is Einstein's Theory of Relativity?

Classical vs. Modern Space and Time

Newtonian mechanics came out of a separation of space, time, and matter, which had not existed in European thinking previously. Early Greeks spoke of four substances called Earth, Water, Fire, and Air and did not recognize space and time as categories separate from substances. Until the time of Descartes—who talked about extended substance in his work, Meditations, published 41 years before Newton—it was assumed that space and time were attributes of substance. Hence, the separation of space, time, and matter was a huge leap forward in Newtonian mechanics.

Newton's calculus depends on the separation of matter, space, and time because it speaks about the motion of an object in space and time and objects can move in space and time only if they are separate from space and time. The separation of space, time, and matter is still commonly assumed today, although these concepts underwent a serious transformation in the early part of the 20th century in Einstein's theories of relativity. In this post, I will describe what Einstein was doing, why he was doing it, and where it eventually led him.

Special Relativity and Logical Positivism

Beginning with the Special Theory of Relativity, Einstein started substituting the word space with the word meter and the word time with the word clock. This was keeping in line with the Vienna school of philosophy called Logical Positivism which was trying to reduce all words to measurements. Logical Positivists wanted to purge philosophy of esoteric words such as beauty, justice, morality, truth, existence, and so on, and transform the meaning of all words to instrument measurable outcomes. The charge against these words was that they were metaphysics, not measurable by physical instruments.

Einstein took a leaf out of Logical Positivism and started applying it to metaphysical words within physics such as space and time. Nobody can see space and time. Even if we talk about distance and duration, which are parts of the metaphysical entities called space and time, we know their meanings through instruments like a meter and a clock. Therefore, Einstein replaced metaphysical words like space and time with the words meter and clock respectively. He wanted to create a Positivist physics free of Newtonian metaphysics.

The Special Theory of Relativity led to two outcomes called *Length Contraction (LC)* and *Time Dilation (TD)*. Since these terms tend to confuse most people, therefore, to understand what they mean, we must substitute the word length with the word meter and the word time with the word clock. LC means that moving meters are contracted (i.e., become smaller). TD means that moving clocks are dilated (i.e., run slower). If we use a contracted meter to measure an uncontracted distance, then the result will be longer. If we use a dilated clock to measure an undilated duration, then the result will be shorter.

This is how Einstein made the formerly objective space and time, or distance and duration, observer-dependent. Two observers—let's call them A and B—can measure the same thing while moving at different speeds. Each observer will get a different value of distance and duration because their meters and clocks are contracted and dilated differently. However, each observer will believe that they are stationary, and thus, they will conclude that their measurements are correct. The result of two measurements by A and B will produce two sets of values on the same reality. Nobody can say which of these two measurements is reality. They are both true and yet mutually incongruent.

General Formulation of Relativity

Each observer could still know if he was accelerating. Einstein removed that possibility by saying that we cannot even know if we are accelerating because the backward force experienced during acceleration can also be caused by a gravitational force. A gravitational force can bend a meter, not just expand or contract it. A gravitational force can bend a clock, not just expand or contract it. Therefore, in the general formulation of relativity—called the General Theory of Relativity—Einstein started talking about curved space and time different from LC and TD. Since these terms may confuse most people, therefore, to understand what they mean, we must replace the word space with meter and the word time with clock. Curved space means that our meter is curved. Curved time means that our clock is curved.

If we measure the world with a curved meter, curved distances will appear straight and straight distances will appear curved. An object may be moving on a curved trajectory but it will seem to be moving on a straight trajectory to some observers (whose meters are curved) and on a curved trajectory to other observers (whose meters are not curved). If we measure the world with a curved clock, objects moving forward may seem to be moving backward, because a curved clock will go slower or faster compared to other clocks. As a result, distances, durations, directions, and angles were all observer-dependent.

The theory of relativity has little to do with metaphysical space and time and everything to do with the measurement of space and time using material instruments like meters and clocks. Since material objects are elongated, compressed, twisted, and bent under the gravitational force, therefore, the result of using them for measurement can also be elongation, compression, twisting, and bending. There was no other meaning to space and time if we restricted ourselves to physics rather than metaphysics.

Observer-Dependent Measurements

While these things were going on in the theory of relativity, there was a parallel development called quantum theory under

which light transformed from waves to particles. A wave uniformly spreads to all locations in space and by that spreading everyone comes to know of the existence of something that emits light. But a particle goes to only one place and we detect the presence of something by detecting a particle of light—called a photon. Thereby, everyone could know the existence of everything when light was a wave. But everyone cannot know the existence of everything when it is a particle. Each observer will occasionally know of the existence of something—if and when a photon arrives at that observer's measuring instrument. Thus, knowing whether something exists also became observer-dependent.

If we combine the principle of relativity with the quantum principle of occasional detection, then there are two measurement problems: (a) each observer in the universe cannot know of the existence of everything, and (b) if and when they know of its existence, what it is, is also observer-dependent.

The reason that quantum and relativity theories could not be combined is because relativity transformed space and time into a *continuous* field and quantum mechanics transformed matter into *discrete* particles. A unified theory requires the same thing to be both continuous and discrete but there is no known method to achieve this at present. The best viable solution is that we quantize space and time, and make locations in space and time discrete particles. However, that will destroy calculus which depends on the smoothness and continuity of space and time.

Einstein's Idealistic Position in Physics

The crucial innovation in relativity theory is that space and time are also matter. However, they are not the kind of matter that we call quantum objects. The former is continuous and the latter is discrete. How can we reconcile these two kinds of matters into a single unified theory without a contradiction?

The answer is easy—treat relativity matter as an observer's *senses* and quantum matter as the observed *objects*. It requires us to say something profound, namely, the words space and time are tied to our senses and constitute the goggles through which we see a quantum word of sensed objects. Einstein came to this profound conclusion when he started talking about Kantian Idealism in which space and time were an observer's "synthetic a priori" categories not objective "realities out in the world". It doesn't mean that objective space and time are absent. It just means that the objective space and time are the metaphysical *noumena* that cannot be known. We can only know the physical *phenomena*.

While Einstein agreed with Kant that space and time were observers' goggles to see the world, he did not agree with the Kantian idea that everyone wore the same type of goggles. In Kantian Idealism, space and time are hardwired categories in our minds and everyone must see the world in the same way. In Einsteinian Idealism, everyone is wearing a different type of goggles. Nobody can say whose goggles are better. For Kant, words like meter and clock have a universal meaning. But for Einstein, meters and clocks can be contracted, elongated, curved, or straightened. The results of the measurements were also different. Nobody can know if their meters and clocks are shorter, longer, curved, or straight. No observation can be said to give us a truer picture of reality. All measurements were now observer-dependent.

Philosophy Lags in Philosophical Terms

Unfortunately, there are no words for the observer-dependent perception of reality in the Western philosophical lexicon. The classical philosophical words are Realism and Idealism. Realism means objective truth and Idealism means subjective truth. There is no word for an objective truth being differently perceived by each observer. Therefore, when we describe physics in ordinary language, we run into the problem that the Western philosophical lexicon does not have the appropriate word for the observer-dependent perception of reality. Some people might therefore incorrectly equate this to pure Idealism while others might think that it is the rejection of any kind of Realism.

Physics is indicating neither pure Realism nor pure Idealism. There is some reality—otherwise, there would be no meaning to science. But the numbers we plug into the equations of science are observer-dependent. Because of quantum theory, every observer may not see everything. Because of relativity theory, every observer may see the same thing differently because their senses are like longer, shorter, curved, or straight meters and clocks. Thus, we reject both pure Idealism and pure Realism.

Religious Origins of Objective Reality

But there is more to the problem than just the absence of a philosophical term for the situation in physics. To understand it, we have to step into the history of Christianity, more specifically, the Biblical claim that all humans are children of Adam and Eve, and they have inherited their sinful nature. Due to their sins, they cannot know the truth on their own and truth can only be known through revelation.

For over 1500 years, after the dawn of Christianity, the idea of sin prevented any rational inquiry into any natural subject. Everything had to be known through the scripture and whatever was not in the scripture was unknowable. Alternatively, even if something was knowable but if God had not given us something in scripture, then He did not want us to know it. Trying to know something that God did not want us to know was an act of defiance.

The problem of sin and evil was solved by John Locke when he said that the human mind was a *tabula rasa* or "blank slate" at birth. We cannot overestimate the importance of these two words because they washed away the inherited sin and evil in Christianity. Every human was now pure and he or she could know the objective truth about the world. All doubts about sense perception accuracy were resolved by saying that we will derive our knowledge of the world through instrument measurements and not sense perception. All doubts about mental cognition were resolved by saying that we are born pure at birth. Thus arose the dogma of objectivity at the dawn of Enlightenment. But it was destroyed in the early 20th century by the advent of quantum and relativity theories. The situation has remained more or less stagnant since—which is close to a century now.

Applying Sāñkhya Concepts to Physics

In Sāñkhya philosophy, both senses and their objects comprise three qualities called sattva, rajas, and tamas. The senses are *continuous* but the sense perceptions are *discrete*. Therefore, if we were looking for something that is both continuous and discrete, then it is the three qualities. These senses constitute our personal space and time, loosely equivalent to Einstein's contracted, elongated, curved, or straight meters and clocks. Our sense qualities contaminate our perception to create a distorted picture of reality. The truth can be known by purifying our senses.

The senses are neither permanently impure as in Christianity nor are they pure at birth as per John Locke. Every observer is not equally impure. The variation in impurity is due to the presence of sattva, rajas, and tamas in the senses. Since this impurity can be removed, therefore, it is possible to know the truth. The relativity of perception is due to impurity and absolutism of perception is due to purity.

The issue of selective perception can also be understood based on qualities. Every observer cannot see everything because the senses contaminated by one quality can only see things in that quality.

However, the impurities in the senses are not constant. The type and extent of impurity in the sense changes with time. A common example in Sāñkhya is seeing the rope as a snake. We don't always see the rope as a snake. We don't always notice the rope. Thereby, the idea of reproducibility in science is also rejected because the instruments (or senses) are changing which changes the results of measurement (or observation). This is well-known via the varying results of measuring the same thing repeatedly. However, experimental sciences disregard all such the variations as instrument errors and environmental changes.

Corresponding to the Lockean idea of *tabula rasa* or "blank slate", there is a process of cleansing the mind in Sāñkhya, called *cheto darpan marjanam*. We aren't born clean slates. Nor are we eternally impure. Everyone is not equally impure. Nor is the impurity constant over time. Different observers have greater or lesser impurities. Even those impurities increase and decrease over time. However, through a process of cleansing, we can obtain a pure mind. When the mind is completely purified, then the objective truth can be known. Until then, the perception is distorted based on the type of impurity in the observer.

Recapitulating the Discussion

Let's summarize all these things discussed thus far into the following easily digestible points:

- Everyone cannot perceive everything that exists due to quantum effects
- Everyone does not see the same thing in the same way due to relativistic effects
- Even one person cannot see the same thing consistently due to time effects
- Our senses are like elongated, shortened, curved, or straight meters and clocks
- The meters and clocks are altered by the presence or absence of matter
- Our senses are also modified based on changes in time, place, and situation
- The modification of the senses depends on the type of impurity in the senses
- But if we purify the senses then everyone can perceive everything consistently
- That unchanging vision of all that exists can be called the absolute truth
- The senses are continuous whereas the sense perceptions are discrete
- Both senses and their perceptions are created from the three qualities
- Using these qualities, we dissolve the continuity vs. discreteness paradox

The Synthesis of Realism and Idealism

When we include senses in the vocabulary of science, then we have to think of dreams as well. During a dream, discrete sense perceptions emerge from the senses. When the dream ends, the sense percepts merge into the senses. An external world is not necessary for sense perception due to the possibility of dreams. However, when an external world affects us—such as during waking—then the process of sense perception must be just like dreaming.

Perception is described as waves in a pond in Yoga philosophy. Yoga Sutra 1.2 states: "The purpose of yoga is to end the modifications of the mind", that are compared to waves in a pond. The pond can generate waves when a stone is thrown into it. Each pond can throw stones into other ponds—which is a sense of action. No pond throws stones into all other ponds—which is why everyone cannot see everything. Each pond is filled with a different liquid and each stone thrown into a pond has a different shape. Accordingly, the waves generated by stone-throwing into a pond are also different. The difference can be attributed both to the stone and the liquid in the pond. The pond is continuous, but the stones are discrete. The resulting waves are also discrete. This pond, stone, and wave theory is Sāñkhya.

The pond is the mind. Its ability to throw stones into other ponds is the senses of action. The mind's ability to receive stones thrown at itself is the senses of knowledge. The ripples in the pond generated by stones thrown into a pond are the perceptions of senses of knowledge. The ripples in the pond that precede the throwing of stones into other ponds are the perceptions of senses of action.

Since there are many ponds, therefore, there is Realism. But because we know these ponds through the waves generated by the stones that they throw at us, therefore, there is Idealism. We are not seeing the other ponds. We are seeing the waves within a pond generated by the stones thrown at the pond by other ponds. Each stone carries an imprint about the pond that threw it. Each ripple in each pond is thus attributed to some external pond that previously threw a stone. This is how it becomes possible to talk about reality through perceptions.

Alternative Conceptions of Space and Time

There is an absolute space and time in the Vedic system that corresponds to the ground that contains various ponds. As new ponds appear and old ponds dry up, this ground for all ponds evolves. Within this absolute space and time are relative spaces and times that correspond to the individual ponds and the ripples in them.

All these ponds are organized hierarchically in an inverted tree structure such that when one pond throws a stone into another pond, the path to the other pond involves several intermediary ponds that lie at higher levels in the inverted tree. We can imagine a situation in which a stone thrown by one pond jumps through several ponds until it lands in the destination pond. The intermediate ponds are demigods. They can absorb the stones thrown by lower-level ponds ensuring that they never reach their destination. They can modify the shape of the stones thrown ensuring that what the receiver sees is different from what was originally thrown. They can also throw stones into ponds creating an illusion of reality or a dream which looks just like when there is actually a reality. The higher-level ponds also get ripples that correspond to their experiences. They can control each lower-level pond's ripples.

Thus, reality is the inverted tree of ponds. The perception is ripples in each pond. We try to guess the reality by perception but it is very hard to know it because the ponds are filled with different liquids and the ripples in them are created by differently shaped stones. To know the reality, we have to purify the liquid in the pond and ensure that stones are not improperly modified in transit. Until that time, we will have perceptions that are not the truth, although they exist. The ripples in a dirty pond exist but they are not the truthful understanding of the inverted tree. Therefore, they are all called illusions. Only the ripples in the purified pond are called the truth. Thus, the world is both existent and yet delusional.

Anti-Realism in Science and in Sāñkhya

This idea of reality is consistent with all the anti-realism found in science. It reconciles what cannot be reconciled in modern science. It is not impersonalism because there are many separate ponds. It is not materialism because the ponds are minds rather than objects. It is not pure realism because the ponds are filled with dirty liquids. It is not pure idealism because the liquid in the pond can be cleaned.

Thus, all the positions are true in one sense and all the positions are false in another sense. The science that emerges out of this conception of reality involves the explanation and prediction of which stones will be thrown out of and into which ponds, and how those stones with either progressively cleanse the pond, or dirty it further. The former is the path to greater truth. The latter is the path to greater falsehood.

An understanding of Einstein's work in relativity and quantum theories is another route to understanding Sāñkhya philosophy. Similarly, those who know Sāñkhya philosophy can also understand the problems indicated by Einstein's work in relativity and quantum theories. If we know the scientific theories, the historical contexts that led to such theories, and the philosophies that motivated them, then the problems and solutions are easy. Without these, a caricature of scientific reality as objective observer-independent truth prevails.

Reinterpreting Relativity as Perception

The senses and the mind are not blank slates. They have innate tendencies. The senses and the mind are not also not interacting with everything in the universe at once. They are selectively, occasionally, and contextually interacting with different things at different times, places, and situations. The resulting perceptual results are far more complex.

Let's apply this to the problem of speed of light measurements, where a beam of light is emitted toward a reflector and the reflected beam is absorbed by the emitter. The delay between the emission and absorption is used to measure the speed of light. But this is a classical physical view of reality. In the quantum view of the same reality, the photons are emitted, absorbed, and reemitted by the "reflector". The time taken in absorption and reemission is not fixed because both involve a probabilistic quantum collapse, which doesn't occur consistently. When the collapse comes earlier or later, the same distance would be divided by a shorter or longer time, and the resulting speed of light will not be constant.

Similarly, let's apply this problem to the measurement of distance to galaxies. If photons arrive slower at the detector, then the detected intensity of light will be lower, which will be interpreted (according to the Inverse Square Law of Luminosity) as greater distance to the galaxy. Conversely, if photons arrive faster at the detector, then the detected intensity of light will be higher, which will be interpreted as shorter distance to the galaxy. Since the photon arrival is not uniform therefore the detected intensities are not uniform and the resulting distance measurements cannot be constant.

Understanding the Problem of Perception

Even to ensure a consistent speed or distance measurement, we have to ensure that the sender and receiver are sending and receiving photons consistently. There is no guarantee for that in quantum theory. The theory is compatible with both consistent and inconsistent emission and absorption of photons. Hence, no measurements are reliably repeatable. Every measurement is unique, and we cannot claim to know reality unless we can guarantee that the senders and receivers are themselves not behaving inconsistently.

LC and TD simply point toward the fact that some types of behaviors are more likely than others in some situations. When an object moves relative to another, the delay in photon arrival is, on average, higher. We might also say that an appearance of motion is created when the photon delay is higher. That higher delay results in time dilation and the clock appears to run slower. The measured reality seems farther from the measuring instrument, and is called length contracted. TD and LC are simply results of changing delay of photon arrival.

Thus, all problems come down to the probabilistic nature of quantum theory where photon emission is not consistent, a photon can be emitted sooner or later, which will then alter the speed and distance measurements, and no experiment can be called repeatable. Unless we understand the mechanisms of quantum emission and absorption, nothing can be said about the truthfulness or falsehood of an empirical measurement.

At present, physics assumes *uniformity* to probabilities over arbitrary chosen durations of time. For instance, if the probability of an event is 0.1, then one such event will occur over 10 smallest units of time measurement, and will remain consistently 10% of events over any arbitrary period of time. This is simply not true. Without this, there is no objectivity or repeatability.

Relativity is about the changing probabilities of events. A moving object is more likely to have delayed photon reception. Due to effects of other objects, some events are more likely to occur than others. All notions of objectivity have been destroyed by relativity and quantum theories. We have to now move toward understanding perception to solve these problems.

Choices in General Relativity

Abstract

While it is well-known that general relativity allows degenerate solutions to the field equations, it is believed that this indeterminism does not have experimental consequences. In this article I argue to the contrary: that current ways of thinking about matter distributions miss one important kind of distribution in which objects can swap the events through which they pass. Under the interpretation that an object is an observer, these distributions amount to different experiences for the same observers. I show that current relativity has no way of distinguishing between these empirically distinct distributions and new concepts of matter are needed to distinguish them. To distinguish such indistinguishable alternatives requires choice. The indeterminism of current relativity can be seen as the choice that decides a matter distribution. Gauge freedom can now be interpreted as a new kind of (empirical) indeterminism in which the events in the universe are determined, but who enacts those events is not. Relativity is 'what' deterministic but 'who' indeterministic. The consequences of this view for our philosophical and physical notions about space-time are explored.

Introduction – The Hole Argument

General relativity (GR) is today formulated in three stages [Norton (2008)]: (1) identify a set of events; also called the manifold of events, (2) distinguish and order the events using a space-time metric; the metric tells us which events are close by and which events are far apart in space or time, (3) distribute matter over the event manifold plus metric structure; the distribution produces world-lines that depict individual moving objects within GR.

Now, the Hole Argument goes as follows. Take a manifold of events and distribute metric and matter fields over it in a smooth way. There are multiple ways of distributing the metric and matter fields over the event manifold (governed by the *gauge freedom*) in relativity. The Hole Argument is the problem that it is possible to identify a small region in space-time in which matter can be smoothly redistributed in such a way as to preserve everything outside the region. This leads to a problem that matter distribution outside the Hole does not determine distribution in the hole and hence relativity is indeterministic.

Einstein originally formulated the argument (given his penchant for thought experiments) as a justification for why general covariance is impossible but later withdrew the argument [Einstein, 1916] echoing a positivist comment of Kretschmann that observations of science must be presented as interaction between objects. This was later rechristened as the *Point Coincidence Argument* of Einstein by John Statchel [1980]. The Point Coincidence Argument says that the intersection of world-lines are unchanged by any smooth re-distribution of matter (the intersection of the world-lines is interpreted as the events of measurement by an observer), and such measurements exhaust the empirical content of theory. So, redistribution of matter mathematically appears to be a different material reality but is empirically of no consequence.

Earman and Norton [1987] first used the Point Coincidence Argument to critique space-time substantivalism. The main criticism [Norton, 1988 & 1989] of the Hole Argument can be summarized as follows. GR allows a gauge freedom subject to certain invariants remaining unchanged. It is the contention of those who critique the Hole Argument that these invariants exhaust the empirical content of the world[1]. Invariants include observables such as the space-time interval, the total mass of the universe, the total energy and momentum, etc. It may be said that these invariants together specify the symmetries of the universe and GR allows multiple possible representations of the universe subject to these invariants remaining unchanged. John Norton [2008, Supplement] compares these representations to different ways of modeling the geography of the Earth. His claim is that just as the surface of Earth can be modeled through different cartographic representations, the manifold of events can also be denoted as many space-times. While the distance between two points in one such model might appear to be larger than another, this is only up to the point that we have not accounted for the 'scale' that must be applied to that representation. However, as an observer goes from one reference frame to another his space-time is stretched or compressed in a way that the invariants remain unchanged. Because these invariants exhaust the empirical content of the theory, the Hole Argument does not tell us anything new empirically.

Arguing the Hole Argument

I will begin the defense of the Hole Argument with a distinction between two kinds of matter redistributing transforms, only the first of which is overtly considered today in the critiques of the Hole Argument (and GR in general). In the present critiques (shown in the first part of Figure-1), a matter redistributing transform is called a diffeomorphism, which globally changes the coordinate *representation* of the manifold similar to that used in different cartographic representations of Earth. This coordinate change can alternately be interpreted as matter redistribution (considering equivalence of active and passive diffeomorphisms[2]) and it follows that the equations of GR are compatible with several matter distributions. Note, however, that in a coordinate change, intersections of world-lines are unchanged and this was the fundamental point of Einstein's argument: the coordinate changes do not tell us anything empirically new about the world.

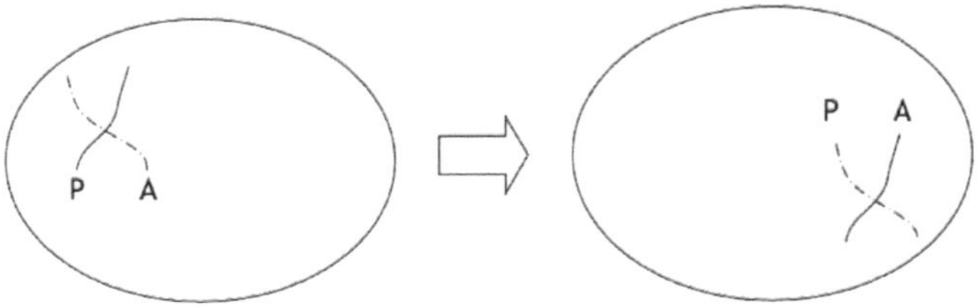

Redistribution of Matter - Just a Coordinate Change

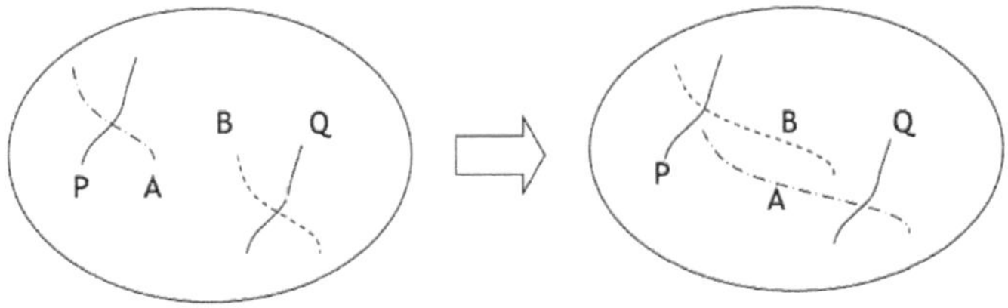

Redistribution of Matter - Identities of Intersecting Objects Different

Figure-1: Two Kinds of Matter Redistributions

Transformations of interest to us in this article instead would be those in which trajectories look different globally but they look identical locally. In the second part of Figure-1, an object 'A' that was earlier involved in a trajectory intersection with object 'P' is after the transformation involved in an intersection with object 'Q'. The reverse has happened for object 'B'. Of course, this change cannot come about by simply a coordinate transformation. It rather involves a matter redistribution. If we simply look at the local intersections of these trajectories, nothing has changed; the intersections remain the same. Given that GR relies on point coincidences, such a matter distribution is eminently allowed. At the point of intersections, the properties of the trajectories (defined by the mass, speed, direction of movement and acceleration of the respective frames of reference) remain unchanged. However, the actual objects inhabiting the frames of reference have changed. It is notable, that the points of intersection can be arbitrarily close to each other, provided there are relevant events at which trajectories are intersecting.

The matter redistributing transforms described here are sometimes called symmetry transforms in mathematics. Let us understand this through an example. Think of an object such as a cube. This object can be described in different coordinate representations—such as spherical and polar coordinates. When I change the coordinate system, I *globally* apply this change to all objects in the space. All diffeomorphic transformations involve global changes. But, there is also a transformation in which I can change the object without having to change coordinates globally. This is for example when I rotate the cube about an axis perpendicular to one of its faces. If the rotation is any multiple of 90^0 then the rotated and the original objects are indistinguishable. The various operations that leave an object indistinguishable from its other configurations are its symmetry operations. Swap of location between two objects of identical mass is a symmetry operation in GR. Present GR has considered diffeomorphic transforms but not symmetry operations, as matter distributions.

The kind of symmetry operation described here involves the swapping of objects of the same *kind*—i.e. with identical properties. For instance, GR cannot distinguish when two masses of 5kg each are swapped between two frames of reference. Indeed, given that we are interested only in Point Coincidences now, a set of objects $\{X_{1,} X_{2,} X_{3\,\ldots} X_N\}$ can be constructed from available matter in various ways. Imagine that I have 10 buckets each with 1 liter of water. Suppose also that I am required to transfer this water into another 10 buckets such that each bucket after the transfer has exactly 1 liter of water. The simplest way to do this is to transfer the water of each bucket directly into another bucket. This would correspond to a diffeomorphic transformation (in which each point in spacetime is mapped to another point after the transformation). But it is also possible to create 1 liter water buckets by 'combining' water from other buckets in many different ways, subject to the conditions that (1) each bucket ultimately has 1 liter of water and (2) the total water in all the buckets put together is 10 liters. The different ways of distributing matter into buckets here is not a diffeomorphic transformation[3] but a symmetry transformation.

Trajectories in classical physics (and GR) are continuous. This means that an object cannot swap its location with another object on another trajectory because it can 'move' only infinitesimally forward on a trajectory that is its own designated path. So, symmetric matter distributions are impossible in classical physics, and by implication it might seem that they are forbidden in GR as well. However, I will argue here that GR is compatible with discrete matter swaps (as opposed to continuous motions in classical physics) because the theory only deals with the total energy of the universe, not its *distribution*. Swapping identical objects preserves the mass, energy, events, and world-lines—the net empirical content of the theory.

In the current way of thinking about world-lines, a world-line evolves in terms of its speed, direction of movement and acceleration. At each point of the world-line, I can attach a frame of reference that defines the speed, direction of movement and acceleration at that point. Now, the world-line can be interpreted in two ways. First, I might say that an object inhabits a particular frame and that frame evolves along with the world-line; so, a world-line is the motion of a frame with an object fixed onto the frame. Second, I might say that each point on a world-line has a frame fixed to it; frames don't evolve; rather, an object 'jumps' from one frame to another. In principle, a jump from one frame to another can be arbitrarily small. In classical physics, I can tend their size of jumps to 0 (through a limit) to achieve the continuity of trajectories. But, in GR, given that I am interested only in point coincidences and point coincidences need not be continuous (indeed, as I will shortly show they cannot be continuous), GR is compatible with the notion that an object actually performs a discrete 'jump' from one line to another. The continuity of trajectories (determinism) follows if I tend the jumps to 0, but as I will show, this is not necessary.

'Jumping' is also consistent with quantum ideas about matter (think of a quantum particle 'moving' in a bubble chamber)—QT does not allow continuous trajectories but allows discrete jumps. If GR has to be reconciled with QT, then the ideas about motion or trajectories must be reconciled prior. Since QT cannot be completed with continuous trajectories (a wavefunction must alternate between measurement 'collapse' and deterministic evolution), evolving our notions about motion in GR makes sense. In particular, converting continuous trajectories to discrete ones in GR is one possible approach to ultimate reconciliation. Further, because the next frame to which an object is going to 'jump' in can be arbitrarily close to the frame from which it is 'jumping' out, the idea of discreteness does not do violence to the general principles of GR. In the present theory, I could think of these points being arbitrarily close by and when I attempt to unify GR with QT, I might then construe that the Planck's constant □ places a limit to the 'size' of these 'jumps'. The change from continuity to discreteness is a major change; fixing the size of these jumps later would be only a matter of degree.

The point of introducing the notion of jumps here is that this allows us to think of matter distribution over the event manifold in an entirely new way. Specifically, if an object has to 'jump' from one frame to another, then it can jump to several different frames. Redistribution of matter can now be compared to objects playing musical chairs – the chair being the trajectory upon which an object 'sits'. In the simplest case, two objects very close by, each having the same mass, can swap locations, quite compatible with GR. In a more complex case, multiple objects can re-divide and swap locations subject to the total mass, energy and momentum remaining conserved. (Indeed, if I apply quantum principles to interpreting GR, I might say that there is indeterminism with regard to which frame the object is going to jump into and hence the next frame of the material object cannot be predicted.) In classical mechanics, this is conceivable only in the case of collisions, when trajectories actually intersect, because then the identities of objects can change due to collisions. But, once I conceive of jumps, it is not necessary that the frames of reference of the object playing musical chairs actually intersect. The trajectories could just happen to be nearby.

While the notion of jumps fits neatly with notions of matter in QT, it does not depend upon them. There are justifications *within* current GR for considering these jumps as valid physical notions. Let us consider these reasons now. Newton's gravitational theory uses continuous trajectories, each point of which is regarded a fact of measurement because an observer in principle continuously observes a trajectory. When we drop the notion of continuous observation in GR[4], we are left with Point Coincidences—the intersection of trajectories. An object now is observed only at the points at which it intersects with other trajectories. So now, the relevant facts for the theory are not continuous trajectories but the points of trajectory *intersections*. While GR still uses continuous trajectories, this use is not necessary with the Point Coincidence Argument in place, unless of course, I insist that a trajectory has infinitely many intersections with other trajectories at infinitely short intervals in a continuous fashion.

GR is consistent with the idea that events of intersection can be arbitrarily close without requiring us that this jump tends to 0 (which is needed for a trajectory to be continuous and bars jumps). In fact, the notion of continuous intersections is inconsistent with practical experience because the interval between trajectory intersections tending to 0 amounts to the use of objects of size 0 which is physically impossible (although classical mechanics and GR postulate it). Point particles of size 0 were used in classical mechanics although no physical objects are actually of size 0. Zero size objects don't create conceptual problems when I have to just draw continuous trajectories but they do create problems when I have to conceive of trajectory intersections. Now, if the intersecting trajectories correspond to finite sized objects, then these intersections must at least leave a gap of the size of the colliding particles for us to be able to identify each intersection as a distinct event. If the events are placed closer than the size of the objects, then events cannot be distinguished. Indeed, I might say that the quantum uncertainty principle has taken us to a logical limit to the divisibility of space-time although within a classical theory such as GR I could merely surmise that there must be a logical limit to divisibility of a trajectory into individual points without actually specifying this limit. In present GR, I am perfectly well off even when I just allow two trajectories to intersect arbitrarily close without tending this distance to 0. In such a case, present-day GR is consistent with the second kind of matter redistributing transformation proposed here.

Giving up continuity of trajectories to retain Point Coincidence only allows us to construe new kinds of matter distribution without violating any physical principles.

Now we might ask: how is the new kind of matter redistribution empirically any different from the first kind? After all, we still have the same Point Coincidences, and thus the events predicted by the theory remain unchanged. The answer is that although events remain unchanged, the participating *objects* in those events are different. In principle, any of these objects could be observers. And when observers are present in one frame and not another, there is a tangible difference to their *personal* experiences.

Frames vs. World-lines

The current space-time perspective in GR is drawn from Special Relativity (SR) in which frames of reference move at constant speeds against each other and an observer essentially looks upon the universe as a bystander who might dispassionately observe the events of the world go by. Because the observer moves at constant speed, and there is no acceleration or gravitation involved, it can be supposed that the observer is indeed mass-less (the mass of the observer has no causal role to play in SR). For, if the observer is massive and he moves through a gravitational field, then, (1) he must accelerate and, in the process, (2) alter the gravitational field in turn. So, the moving frames of SR are mass-less goggles. And because they are mass-less they are causally outside the world. If we apply the perspective of SR to interpret GR, it leads to the premise that frames of reference in GR are different perspectives, quite like those of the moving observers in SR. Thus, an observer uses a frame of reference as he was accelerating although the observer stands outside the manifold of events. This is essentially how GR is constructed today. Thus, in step (2) of the formulation of GR given in the Introduction, I distribute metric fields upon the manifold—a metric that applies globally—from the perspective of an observer that stands outside the manifold. Obviously, if there is a metric, there must be an observer. And if the metric corresponds to an accelerating frame, then the observer too must accelerate. But, the observer in this case is outside the manifold and therefore is also mass-less (his mass has no causal role to play). Two problems can now be raised. First, how can a mass-less observer accelerate? Second, can there even be a mass-less observer?

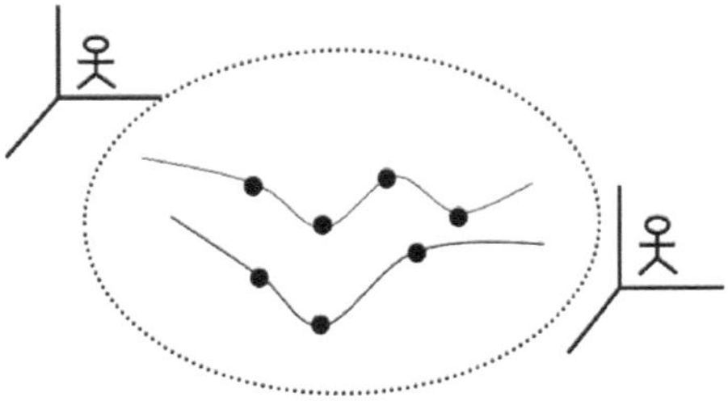

frames in special relativity - causally outside the physical world

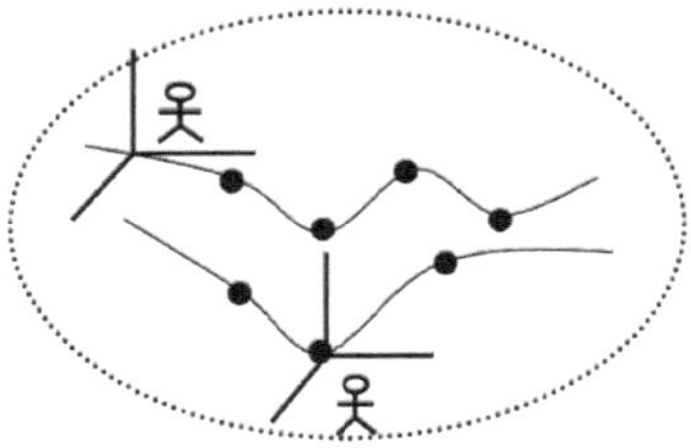

frames in general relativity - causally inside the physical world

Figure 2: Observation Frames in SR and GR

The above two questions are rhetorical. In the present theory, answers to both are in the negative and this just goes to show that there cannot be mass-less frames of reference that *accelerate*. All observers must be massive and therefore observers must be causally inside the world and not outside of it[5]. Now, when an observer is a massive object inside the world, his space-time pertains to a trajectory rather than the global space-time. That is, unlike in SR where space-time included the observation of all objects (because the observer was outside the world and looked upon it) in GR, an observer can observe only the events with which he interacts. These interactions are identical to the observer's world-line. This requires us to collapse the distinction between a frame of reference and a physical object. The fact that GR allows frames of reference to accelerate introduces the case when real *massive* observers can observe the world (instead of the mass-less goggles of SR). Now, I can say that the very reason a frame is accelerating is because the observer in it is massive (it requires us to treat every physical object as an observer, and although this is an extreme thought it is compatible with GR). While in SR, frames were 4-dimensional massless goggles, these must now be treated as world-lines in GR. Each world-line is a space-time frame as the observer who observes the world from his vantage point.

It follows that a collection of world-lines is not only multiple different objects but also simultaneous different perspectives about the world because each object is now a distinct (accelerating) frame of reference. Because all observers are massive and all observers are within the world, each observer must bring a different space-time view in which the laws of nature are true. Each of these space-times is a simultaneously true representation of the world. Coordinate transforms are not about a hypothetical scenario when observers *could* accelerate and observe the manifold of events while standing outside the world (like they used to in SR). In GR, to even accelerate, an object must be inside the world as one of the objects. In this view, different coordinate systems are (1) the ability to regard each object in the world as an observer with its own frame of reference and (2) the ability to cut up the manifold of events into different trajectories. Figure-2 shows how a massive observer must exist causally inside the world and not outside it. Now, the number of possible frames of reference at any point in time equals the number of objects in the manifold (each object carries with it its own perspectival space-time). Hence, an observer gains new experiences by being in a different frame and matter distribution over different frames leads to new experiences.

World-lines vs. Objects

Now, this might appear to be a mysterious issue associated with consciousness, but it is not. This issue rather relates to the fact that when GR draws world-lines, a frame of reference is not explicitly associated with an individual object but only with an object of a certain *kind*. A frame of reference just defines a *role* in which a particular object (observer) can step in. Roles are merely objects of a certain *kind*—for example, I might say that trajectory X is an object of 5 kg moving at 10 meters per second. By cutting up the world into roles I am merely stating which *kinds* of objects I want in the universe. There can be several objects that have the mass of 5 kg and the frame is compatible with any of them inhabiting it. Now, it is apparent that the fact that an object is capable of inhabiting different frames of reference is just how classical mechanics is designed. Here, an object can have many different velocities and acceleration (the different reference frames). So, how is the problem of consciousness now being introduced? How do I physically decide that an observer goes into one frame and not another? Without going into details I might just suggest that newer ways of distinguishing objects are needed to account for this new problem; these ways must allow us to distinguish between two objects that each weighs 5 kg. We can also suspect that these newer ways might come from QT since all objects (fermions) in QT are distinct. So, if I were to look upon two masses of 5 kg each, quantum theoretically, there would indeed be a distinction between them. The distinction between the experiences of two objects in two different frames is in everyday parlance a fact of consciousness. But this fact requires having a material correlate. GR does not have this correlate, so the correlate must come from elsewhere.

In terms of present GR, I may just draw a distinction between a frame and an object, which I have already made when I said than an object hops through frames. While at this point the ability to hop to one frame rather than another appears as an indeterminism within GR, this indeterminism can be looked upon as opening up the need for newer ways to distinguish objects within GR and hence provides us with a reason to look for a synthesis with QT from within the confines of GR. Such a justification is not present in GR today because the theory by itself appears complete; there are no *theoretical* reasons for looking to unify GR with QT apart from attaining a unified theory (which is a human reason). The indeterminism of GR can rather be looked upon as the reason why a synthesis with another theory is even required. If the unity with QT does solve the problem of indeterminism, I would say that the quantum and observational reasons for distinguishing between identical masses entering different frames are really the same. Or, that, the differences in the experiences of an object resulting from its presence in a particular frame of reference can be attributed to its quantum theoretic distinction from other objects. In other words, quantum gravity would bring us closer to thinking of material objects as conscious observers. This might be called a quantum gravitational approach to the problem of consciousness. In current similar approaches, Penrose [2004, 2007] proposes the unity as a method by which gravity 'collapses' the quantum wavefunction into a definite state. Instead, I propose the unity as a method by which quantum theory distinguishes identical objects in different frames of reference in GR. In Penrose's approach, GR is deterministic and it overcomes the indeterminism of QT. In our approach, GR itself is indeterministic but in a way that can complement the indeterminism of QT.

Indeterminism in GR

The key point of GR in the context of new kinds of material distributions is the following. When an object accelerates (because of force or because it changed its identity or both), it goes over different events than it would have if it was not accelerating and this modifies the events other observers go over as well. The invariance of properties in GR entails that when an object changes course, it must cause changes in other objects such that some other object now passes over the event that was forsaken by the object that was originally supposed to have passed through it. In other words, GR allows us the freedom to redistribute the matter in the world such that when one object changes course, other objects co-vary with it. The total set of events and their empirical instantiation (the space-time coincidences) remains unchanged. But, the empirical instantiation of events is now enacted by different material objects than before. An event in the world can be multiply realized through various different objects passing over the same events. When different material objects realize the same events, it leads us to a new kind of indeterminism.

Think of two hungry people at a table, with only one ice-cream in front of them. One of the two individuals can eat the ice-cream and if the first one doesn't, the second would definitely. These two possibilities are identical as far the events are concerned (namely, that someone eats the ice-cream). However, they are not identical with regard to the distribution of matter—who actually eats the ice-cream? Both possibilities are identical in terms of intersection of the world-lines, the so-called empirical content of GR. But this empirical content is global and not individual. While the global empirical content remains unchanged (someone eats the ice-cream) the individual empirical content changes—one of the two individuals eats the ice-cream. In GR, this can be represented by two space-time frames. In the first frame, the observer sees himself eating the ice-cream and in the second frame, the observer sees his partner eating the ice-cream. But which observer is in which frame? Relativity is compatible with either of the observers being in any of the frames and this is the indeterminism. The universe is deterministic in that it defines two *roles* or frames of reference one of which eats the ice-cream while the other merely observes. But the universe is not deterministic with regard to which object is in which reference frame. It follows that *what* will happen in the universe is fixed but *who* will participate in it is not. Figure-3 illustrates this indeterminism.

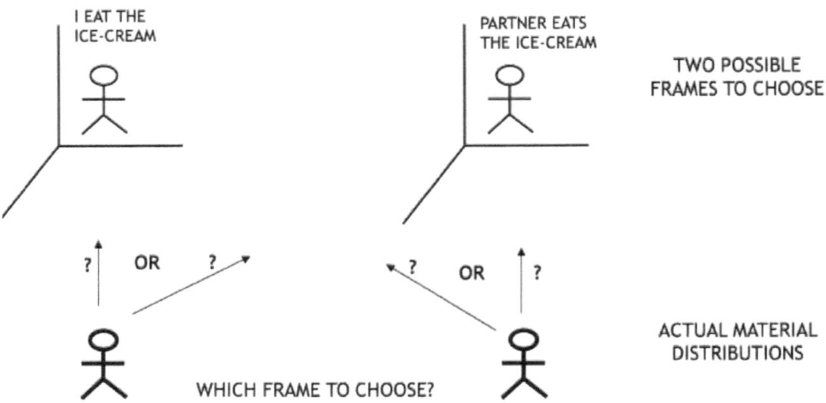

Figure-3 Dilemma of the Ice-Cream Baiters

There are two ways in which to look at indeterminism. The first way is about how I draw trajectories in the manifold of events. This involves connecting various events in the manifold and there are several distinct ways of doing it. Notably, these event connections may not necessarily indicate the evolution of the *same* object—like they used to in classical mechanics (in which the identity of an object did not change while moving). When matter is redistributed, an object's identity (mass in the case of GR) might change as it goes through different events. In the ice-cream case, it corresponds to whether the event of ice-cream eating is enacted by the customers or by the ice-cream vendor himself. In one case, the eating of ice-cream is preceded by people driving to the vendor and being served on tables. In the second case, the eating of ice-cream might be preceded with ice-cream vendor type of activities such as serving a customer ice-cream or collecting their payments. Different *kinds* of trajectories can therefore pass over the same event. The second way is about which actual instance of identically looking ice-cream cones is actually served to a particular customer. This difference is not seen if I just look at the different frames (the possibilities of whether or not a person eats the ice-cream or which particular cone he eats) because different frames are different perspectives about the world (the different objects in the world). The difference is rather evidenced by deciding upon which object inherits which frame of reference because then the other objects must inherit other frames of references. The two ways of seeing indeterminism are the same—namely, which object passes over an event. In the present case, there are two objects passing—the ice-cream and the ice-cream eater—and both are subject to the same indeterminism.

Now, one might ask: if GR is indeterministic why hasn't this been empirically discovered? And the reason is that current relativity does not *a priori* specify the manifold of events. So, when I try to confirm the theory using experiments, a variation in some individual observations can be attributed either to indeterminism in the theory or to a different manifold of events. In the case of current GR, I would do the latter. So, I would say that the universe passes through the observed events because the universe must deterministically pass through these events (which, however, could not have been known *a priori* because I don't know the exact set of events in the world). However, as I have argued in this article, the actual flow of matter over these events is based upon *choice* (theoretically it is a symmetry between different distributions) and the observations reaped depend upon the choices made. It is also possible to argue that choices are not apparent, because changes to world-lines are caused by the gravitational force, which is quite a weak force. So, it might be concluded that large galaxies have a tangible freedom but I as an individual do not. Although it is outside the scope of this article, I can speculate, that this is where the reconciliation of relativity with quantum theory becomes important. As is known, quantum theory deals with the electromagnetic, weak and strong forces while relativity deals with gravity. It is the forces under quantum theory that govern most of everyday objects (almost nothing in modern technology has anything to do with relativity). It has often been supposed that relativity being a deterministic classical theory is contrary to quantum theory, owing to the nature of indeterminism faced in quantum theory. It might instead be said that both theories are indeterministic and this makes their reconciliation that much easier. Of course, this means that I would need to introduce new causal mechanisms by which indeterminism in the joint theory can be overcome but that is a step that I might take for achieving the unity. Before that, it would also be necessary to reformulate GR along the lines of the new kind of construction proposed in this article (equating frames of reference with world-lines; applying not a single metric but multiple metrics simultaneously to the manifold of events).

Reinterpreting Relativity

When currently GR distributes metric and matter fields over the manifold it does create world-lines but all these world-lines are in a single space-time. We don't put each of the objects in different space-times because I don't think of them as observers. But, the space-time in which all the world-lines exist is drawn from the perspective of an observer who is mass-less and not part of the observation. This is the classic mind-matter divide in which the masses are not observers and observers don't have a mass. When an observer positioned outside the world performs a frame transform, he would only change the coordinate *representation* of the world-lines without changing their identities. This can lead to someone (correctly) arguing that the Hole Argument does not entail new experiences. Such changes are indeed akin to various cartographic representations of the Earth's geography [Norton, 2008]. This is because new experiences only come about when someone performs a frame transform being *inside* the world. In this case, an object's changing frame of reference can mean that an object is now jumping through a different set of frames. A change in the association between matter and frames of reference is a symmetry operation that redistributed matter in a way that GR cannot discriminate.

The empiricism of events does not exhaust the total empirical content of the world; there are facts such as which world-lines pass over which events, and which objects inhabit which world-lines which are not explained by GR. GR is in fact totally compatible with different distributions of matter, each of which results in a different history of the universe, and this is the indeterminism. The history of the universe is not just the events that occur in it but also which material objects pass over those events. There is a clear empirical difference between various alternatives in which a particular object passes over an event and when it does not pass over that event because the object passing over the events can itself be the observer.

The difference between SR and GR can be obvious to a super-observer[6] who sits in the manifold of events (and not on a particular world-line) and can see the various distributions of world-lines over the events. Such an observer would be *a priori* unable to decide which course the universe would take. The indeterminism of relativity isn't a hypothetical one, and this is apparent from the position of a super-observer. GR is compatible with the universe following different courses of matter distribution, while preserving the events. Whereas SR is about possibilities of observing the world differently from different individual perspectives, GR is about various possibilities in the perspective of the super-observer himself.

Space-Time Substantivalism

Prior the advent of SR, the 4-dimensional Euclidean space-time was regarded to be the universal container in which the world exists. But, with the advent of SR itself, it became difficult to hold this viewpoint. If there is a unique space-time, then why do different observers observe different lengths and durations from moving frames? Indeed, the notion of the constant speed of light is generally taken to be the refutation of the existence of any plenum in which things exist. But, now, GR throws up new possibilities. In particular, given that all individual space-time perspectives are derived by overlaying a metric and matter structure over the event manifold, I might be tempted to think of the event manifold as the universal space-time [Earman & Norton, 1987]. Because the metric carries the matter and energy, this metric can be considered the contents as opposed to the container of the space-time events.

But, keep in mind that the metric distributed over the manifold of events (the steps 2 & 3 in the construction of GR) are carried out from the perspective of an observer outside the manifold and these therefore don't pertain to the observed intervals. The observed intervals are the distances between events along the world-lines, since every observation event is on the world-line itself. How then do I determine the distances between different world-lines? The answer is that nothing in the perspectival space-time can give us that distance. Perspectival space-time is created at the time of an observation and only gives us the distances between events on the same world-line; it does not give us the interval between the events on different world-lines. The *a priori* 'distance' between events in the manifold (before matter is distributed on these events) must therefore be defined in some other yet unknown way. Because to even redistribute matter over the manifold of events I need a metric and because the perspectival metric is defined only after matter has been distributed (at least objects of a certain *kind* have been identified), there must be another way of distinguishing events in the manifold *before* matter is distributed upon these events. We can call this new metric the *noumenal metric* as opposed to the *phenomenal metric* of the perspectival space-time which describes the observed intervals.

Because the event manifold is fixed and objects of the world cover this event manifold, the *noumenal metric* is a fixed set of intervals between the events. Of course, this is not necessarily how an individual observer sees these intervals since in principle, the trajectory of an object is not fixed, but determined run-time when the object passes over certain events. It is evident to us from everyday experience that when multiple objects pass through different events, they create a distinction between events. The distinction between different events—at any instance in time—is precisely the distinction between objects. And since different material objects can pass over the same events, we might say that the spatial distinction between events is given at the point of matter distribution over events. The *noumenal metric*—it can be surmised—is purely a time-like metric between events. We might look upon the manifold of events plus this time-like metric as a fixed 'script' through which the universe evolves. The script describes events but not the actors. And this is precisely the indeterminism of relativity theory.

The manifold of events and its associated metric can be viewed as an ontological reality, which is translated into phenomena. In an actual history, this ontological reality is known, and the knowledge of reality could vary from one history to another depending upon which objects pass through which events. So, the event ontology does not fix the history, but only constrains it. When an event is enacted by different objects, knowledge of which object has enacted an event changes but the event itself remains unchanged. The perspectival space-time is a moving world-line and that moving observer views (parts of) the event manifold from his perspective; it is created at the point of measurement and this space-time which goes with the observer. The perspectival space-time is relative but the manifold of events and *noumenal metric* are universal.

I don't intend here to suggest that the space-time manifold is a plenum, thing or object (the conventional ways of thinking of ontology). The manifold is rather like the script of a drama that doesn't yet have any actors. New ways of conceiving ontology are needed to accommodate this view. In particular, we are talking about the script of the universe independent of the actors in it. The actors can see the script and then *choose* to participate in it.

When someone looks at a desert and envisions a grand city in its place, he is 'seeing' although not experiencing in the phenomenal sense of having sensations. We constantly 'see' the world as possibilities for the future. In that sense, the manifold of events is not a sensation (until matter is distributed over events) and yet it is known as an imminent possibility. The manifold of events becomes a sensation at the point of observation. This comes very close to views about matter in QT in which reality is said to be 'created' at the point of experience, by the act of measurement, and this could prove helpful when conceiving of a unified theory of quantum gravity. That GR enables a similar viewpoint as QT might be the element of surprise for many. And yet, with the foregoing discussion it is possible to see GR as dealing in the script of a drama while QT deals with the actors which participate in the script. The separation between an actor and a role gives us the intuitive basis to reconcile two formidable theories—QT and GR. But it also introduces a new type of ontology in which the universe has a *destiny* or script quite separate from the freedoms of choices each individual enjoys.

References

- Earman, John and Norton, John (1987) 'What Price Spacetime Substantivalism? The Hole Story', *J. Phil. Set.* 38 (1987), 515-525
- Einstein, Albert (1916), 'The Foundation of the General Theory of Relativity' in H.A. Lorentz *et al.*, *The Principle of Relativity*, New York: Dover, 1952, pp. 111-164.
- Norton, John, 'The Hole Argument', *The Stanford Encyclopedia of Philosophy* (Spring 2008 Edition), Edward N. Zalta (ed.), URL = <http://plato.stanford.edu/entries/spacetime-holearg/>.
- Norton, John D. (1987), 'Einstein, the Hole Argument and the Reality of Space', in John Forge (ed.), Measurement, Realism and Objectivity, Dordrecht: Reidel, pp. 153-188.
- Norton, John D. (1988), 'The Hole Argument', in A. Fine and J. Leplin (eds.), PSA 1988, Volume 2, pp. 56-64.
- Penrose, R. (2004), Shadows of the Mind: A Search for the Missing Science of Consciousness, (Oxford University Press).
- Penrose, R. (2007), The Road to Reality: A Complete Guide to the Laws of Nature, (Vintage Books).
- Stachel, John (1980), 'Einstein's Search for General

Covariance', in Don Howard and John Stachel (eds.), *Einstein and the History of General Relativity* (Einstein Studies, Volume 1), Boston: Birkhäuser, 1989, pp. 63-100.

Notes

[1] I will later dispute this contention. I will argue that invariants exhaust the empirical content of present GR although not of the world when material objects are also observers.

[2] The difference between active and passive diffeomorphisms can be understood by the following example. Imagine that all continents on the surface of Earth are clockwise rotated without rotating the Earth itself and without changing the distances between continents. This is Active Diffeomorphism. Contrast it to the case when the Earth itself is rotated counter-clockwise, while leaving the continents intact. This is Passive Diffeomorphism. It is easy to see how Active and Passive Diffeomorphisms are equivalent. In fact, given their equivalence, it might be hard to see why they should be distinguished. The picture gets slightly more complicated when the coordinate transformation also involves time because then, in the Passive case, the continents are at a new location at time T+1 whereas in Active case they are at the new location at time T itself.

[3] Diffeomorphic transformations are bijective (one-to-one) and differentiable, which the distribution of water is not since the water distribution can be one-to-one, many-to-one or one-to-many.

[4] Now the observer itself must be an object and must have its own trajectory. When an observer observes, trajectories intersect. To suggest that an observer continuously observes an object (which is the premise in classical physics) two trajectories must continuously intersect – or practically speaking – must be congruous all over. The notion of continuous observation can therefore be replaced with at-an-instance observation without losing empirical validity. Now, at the times when an observer observes, his trajectory intersects with the observed world.

[5] This point is further important because Gauge invariance pertains to local symmetries and not global ones. Global invariances correspond to an observer outside the world who observes the world but does not itself have physical properties – e.g. mass. This idealization is misconstrued because all observation involves a physical interaction, and for that to happen the observer must also have physical properties, quite like the objects he observes. This essentially reduces an observer to a physical object (at least from the standpoint of empirical measurements) and the interaction between the observer and the objects is a local interaction based on transfer of energy. The observer can't know the world globally unless the real-world specifies an energy transfer from every object in the world into a single observer-object.

[6] Such a super-observer is a hypothesis, introduced merely to illustrate the distinction between SR and GR.

Endogenous Retroviruses as the Seeds of Self-Destruction

What is an Endogenous Retrovirus?

A retrovirus is a type of virus that inserts its DNA into the host's DNA after which the host begins replicating the virus DNA along with the host's DNA, thus creating copies of the virus alongside copies of its cells. During the CoVID pandemic, there was a fear that the coronavirus vaccine could infect the human cells, making the coronavirus a retrovirus—i.e., part of the human DNA after which human cell replication will either automatically produce the virus in the body or affect the body in other adverse ways. An Endogenous Retrovirus (ER for short) is a type of virus (a) whose DNA was inserted in a host (such as human) DNA, (b) the inserted DNA was inherited through the successive generations of the host, and (c) the inserted DNA resembles the DNA of Exogenous or externally found viruses.

Since the same DNA is found internally and externally for an ER, it is presumed that at some time in history the exogenous virus infected the host DNA, and the host accepted the exogenous virus DNA as part of its own, and began transmitting it through hereditary reproduction. In principle, we could also hypothesize the reverse—namely, that the virus DNA originated in the host DNA, separated from the host at some time in history, and became an exogenous organism with the host as its parent.

However, to hold this reverse hypothesis, we have to show that the ER is *useful* to the host in some way. For example, many bacteria assist our digestion. Some bacteria fight infections. Given their usefulness to the human host, there is no problem in saying that the host is the parent of the bacteria and the bacteria exists outside the host because the host's body excretes waste that carries the bacteria produced by the parent host. In short, the bacteria could be externalized by the host after producing it, rather than being internalized after having been produced externally. The distinction rests on asking: Is the bacteria useful to the human host? However, if we find that the bacteria are harmful to the body, then we would prefer to think that these were produced externally, infected the human host at some time in history, and then became part of the host's DNA. We don't like to think that the host can produce its own nemesis.

Germs vs. Spontaneous Generation

This hypothesis has a lot to do with the *germ theory* of disease in which a pathogen (a nemesis of the host) infects the host to cause disease. The germ theory arose in response to the theory of spontaneous generation of disease. Experiments were conducted on food items by putting them in open and closed jars. It was found that the open jars over time acquired maggots while the closed jars did not. The germ theory then said that if maggots were being spontaneously generated from food, then they would be produced even in closed jars. The claim overlooked the possibility that some diseases could be caused by external originating germs while other diseases can be caused by spontaneous generation in the host.

The germ theory has held sway over biology ever since. It is assumed that the host will never give birth to its nemesis. The germ theory of disease lies at the root of the ER hypothesis too: The viruses cannot be produced within the host but if a virus DNA exists within a host then it must be due to an infection. Modern medical science rests on the germ theory. Under this theory, great emphasis is laid on drugs that kill the germs rather than on leading such a life that will not spontaneously generate the disease.

The traditional systems of medicine do not agree with the germ theory. They emphasize leading a life that never spontaneously produces germs, and never allows the germs (if they exist externally) to live in the body. Thus, two broad schools of medicine exist at present—(a) the first emphasizes leading a life that doesn't spontaneously generate disease and kills the germs if they happen to enter the body, and (b) the second that marginalizes leading a healthy life to prevent spontaneous generation of diseases and emphasizes killing germs. Given the emphasis on the germ theory of disease, the presence of ER in a host DNA is always interpreted as the infection of an endogenous germ into the host rather than its spontaneous generation within, when both could be equally good explanations of observed facts.

Endogenous Retrovirus and Evolution

Modern evolutionary theory assumes that bacteria and viruses preceded humans and progressively led to humans rather than humans generating viruses and bacteria endogenously. The modern theory of evolution is not conceptually consistent with the germ theory of disease because if human DNA evolved from virus DNA, then we should accept that the human DNA must contains the virus DNA as its parental DNA, precisely as the result of evolution from viruses. The question of retroactive infection should not arise when the thing supposedly infecting us is actually the parent from whom we have evolved. We should rather consider the presence of virus DNA in our DNA as a natural sign of evolution from viruses.

The ER hypothesis rests on a contradiction—(a) humans evolved from viruses but they must not contain the virus DNA, and (b) the virus DNA must retroactively infect the human DNA instead of carrying it natively as a result of evolution. This is because the germ theory requires us to say that the viruses are external to humans while evolutionary theory requires us to say that viruses preceded humans.

In contrast stands an alternative idea in which humans did not evolve from viruses but created them endogenously because many viruses serve useful purposes in the host. A host could also generate harmful viruses internally due to spontaneous generation, if it doesn't live in the way that nature created it to live. Such an explanation would refute both germ and evolutionary theories, without contradicting the available evidence. This explanation also doesn't suffer from the contradiction between germ and evolutionary theories under which humans evolved from viruses but cannot natively contain parental virus DNA, which must be retroactively added to the human DNA through an infection by the virus.

The Use of ER for Justifying Evolution

Under the prevailing dogmas of germ and evolutionary theories, ER are used to justify evolution. One such justification begins by saying that the ER DNA is found in both human and ape DNA. The evolutionist claims that this is because ER infected the apes, humans evolved from the apes, and therefore, they must have infected the apes before evolution. They do not say that *all* species evolved from viruses, so the virus DNA must be present endogenously in all species, because it is not true.

Since biology and medicine have rejected spontaneous generation, therefore, they cannot say that viruses are generated in the ape and human body because they are useful to the body. They also cannot accept the idea that the body can generate harmful viruses if the body deviates from its intended way of living created by nature. Instead, research is directed toward proving germ and evolutionary theories when their opposites are also proven by the same data because data underdetermines the theory.

The Presence of ER Without Evolution

The same data can be explained by an alternative theory which is also fundamentally opposed to germ and evolutionary theories. The explanation would say that ER can be spontaneously generated in the body either because they are useful to the body or because harmful germs are spontaneously generated within organisms that deviate from their intended state. Infection by virus is not necessary if germ theory is not the only way to get diseases. A better explanation is that germs are created in a host body when the host deviates from its intended state, are then externalized through excretion, and then infect other hosts if they too have deviated from the intended state and lost the resistance to such infections.

The added benefit of the above alternative theory is that it doesn't suffer from the logically paradoxical claim that humans and apes evolved from viruses but must not carry the parental DNA. The alternative is free from the problem that all species—having evolved from some common virus DNA—do not contain that virus DNA endogenously. Therefore, it is true that data underdetermines the theory if we pick data selectively. However, if we happen to pick all the data, then a false theory can be easily falsified.

Alternative Evolutionary Foundations

The theory of spontaneous generation requires an alternative conceptual foundation in which the seeds of self-destruction lie dormant in all hosts. These inactive seeds are activated spontaneously if the host deviates from its intended state and starts behaving in ways that it is not supposed to. The activation of inactive seeds is the method of self-correction in each host—if it deviates, it is destroyed from within. External causes may facilitate such self-destruction if the host has already been weakened due to the activation of self-destructive seeds within. Such self-destructive seeds may also be externalized to infect other hosts after they have been activated within a host that is deviated from its intended state.

This alternative conceptual foundation of self-destruction cannot be formalized in an axiomatic system of reasoning because rational inference from axioms never lead to a self-contradiction. Axiomatic systems are refuted by something external to them—e.g., empirical evidence that invalidates the axioms. If the external evidence is missing, then the axiom system can never be refuted. But such is not the fate of a rational system which has *intentionality* built into it. An intentional system measures the deviation between the intended and actual states and self-destructs if it has deviated from the intended state.

An intentional system explains the extinction of species in a new way—the species exist so long as they are not deviated from their intended state. But if they deviate, intentional logic activates the dormant seeds of self-destruction and the deviated organism self-destructs. The environment may facilitate that destruction but the core cause of destruction is that the species has deviated from its intended state. Without such deviation, the species will adapt to environmental changes, even if they occur. It will not be destroyed by such environmental changes. However, with the deviation, the organism is weakened from within, becomes incapable of adapting to environmental changes, and is destroyed by it.

This model of biological evolution is consistent with social evolution. A society is supposed to live a moral life. But if a society as a whole becomes immoral, then it activates exceptionally immoral elements within itself that attack the society from within. The society is then hollowed out from inside due to internal conflict between an exceptionally immoral core attacking the mostly immoral society at large. The society that was previously winning against its external foes is now destroyed from within due to the activation of exceptionally immoral and degraded people attacking the society from within. This is sometimes called chickens coming home to roost—the past mistakes come to haunt a society.

The Problem of Collective Evolution

Let's suppose we are living in the early 1900s and seat belts are just being invented. Due to their benefits, every car maker is required to add seat belts to their cars. Let's assume for the moment that there is no patent system hindering the use of common seat belts. As a result, as soon as the seat belt mandate comes into effect, all the cars suddenly have seat belts. The cars did not evolve from one common car. But they got a common car ingredient, namely, a seat belt. This is the evolution of cars, and yet, it is not the evolution of one car from another. It is rather the collective evolution of cars.

Now let's fast forward a few decades to a time when every car is driven by software and there is a system of car driving integrated with road signals and the car positioning system. Assume that this system becomes mandatory because it drastically improves car safety and eliminates the mandatory use of seat belts. The cars still carry seat belts but they become vestiges of the past. This is again the evolution of cars, but not the evolution of one car from another. It is the collective evolution of cars.

While adding a seat belt to a car, in theory, there are millions of potential placements of the seat belt. But if we were intending to make something useful, then we will always put the seat belt on the seat and not anywhere else. The millions of other possible locations of seat belts are just theoretical possibilities. They can be used for a likelihood calculation under the false assumption that seat belts and seats are not related. If they are related, then millions of possible locations of seat belts reduce to just one.

Applying Collective Evolution to ER

We can extend this example to ER. They are like seat belts. At some time, they can collectively appear in different species, which are the counterparts of cars in our example. At yet another time, they may collectively become vestiges of the past. The similarity of the location of the virus DNA shouldn't be a surprise if we know that DNA corresponds to a seat belt expected to be on a seat and nowhere else.

An assumption in modern evolutionary theory is that things happen randomly and too many random events constitute an unlikely coincidence. The same DNA appearing in many species at once is such an unlikely event. To avoid this unlikeliness—assuming that all events are equally likely—evolutionary theory postulates the random appearance of a mutation followed by its gradual inheritance. A theory thus appears to (a) assume large number of possibilities, and (b) selection of one such possibility.

However, we cannot get rid of coincidences like this. For example, a Cambrian Explosion is already known to be an unlikely coincidence. It is when thousands of species are co-created to live together in an ecosystem and form the cycles of nutrients such as food, water, and air. A species cannot survive in isolation. A species always exists in an ecosystem. Species evolution must therefore occur alongside ecosystem evolution, which means the collective evolution of species. This collective evolution of species is like the collective evolution of cars, road signaling systems, car positioning systems, and so forth. It brings a compatibility between species due to which they coexist in an ecosystem. A core aspect of that compatibility is that they collectively agree to follow one system of norms, standards, and rules.

We can call this a collective evolution driven by an intended state of an ecosystem. Just as the cars need not evolve from one another, similarly, species need not evolve from one another. They can co-evolve as part of an ecosystem. This is evolution without evolutionary theory under which events are random. Now, evolution brings large coincidences, such as the collective appearance of seat belts in cars.

Necessity and Sufficiency of Theories

A theory should be accepted if its explanation is necessary and sufficient. Evolutionary theory gives a sufficient but not a necessary explanation. Yes, if species evolved from one another then they could share virus genes. But that could also happen if species evolved collectively. It could also happen if each species carries the seeds of self-destruction within. Each explanation is sufficient but neither is necessary at this juncture. The necessity comes from the recognition of additional facts: (a) Cambrian Explosion type scenarios in which many species appear at once, (b) the absence of the same virus DNA in all species supposedly evolved from them, and (c) the activation of previously inactive hereditary DNA governed by factors innate to an organism or unique to the environment (sometimes called epigenetics). As more factors are collected and integrated, theories with flawed assumptions begin to fall apart.

Therefore, we don't have to be opposed to evolution. We can just be opposed to evolutionary theory. Evolution is data and a theory is the explanation of that data. There is enough data now to rule out Neo-Darwinian evolutionary theory. A different theory is required to explain the data. For instance, (a) the theory must explain rapid explosion of species, (b) the extinction of species, (c) the presence of inactive DNA which can be selectively activated, (d) the presence of similar DNA across multiple species, etc.

But mainstream biology will not accept alternative theories because it is materialistic and reductionistic by definition. Matter cannot have intentionality. Ideas and purposes appear late in the evolutionary cycle. Axiomatic systems are the only type of logical system. Commonalities between species must mean evolution from one species to another rather than a commonality that appears simultaneously or always existed within the species either because it is useful to multiple species or because it is an agency of self-destruction upon deviation from an intended state. The materialism and reductionism of biology is not unique to biology. It is the all-pervading theme of modern science. It the lens through which science looks at the world, interprets the data, and cherry-picks data to claim universality of its chosen lenses.

The institutionalization of materialism, reductionism, and axiomatic reasoning, along with the rejection of every other rational alternative, has nothing to do with nature, reality, life, or truth. It is simply the worldview of people who agree to be parts of that institution so long as it benefits them. Their loud voices proclaiming evolutionary theory indicate their fear that anything that hurts their institution, or the mere presence of an alternative worldview, will rapidly undermine their prestige and power.

Abrahamic Attitudes Toward Evolution

The reason that Abrahamic religions are so riled up about any kind of evolution (not just a specific theory of evolution) is that it contradicts their theology. For example, the historical Western definition of a human is very narrow. At one time, it meant people of Europe. Under Greek and Roman influence, Africans were considered non-human. Due to Judeo-Christianity, women were considered non-human. Africans and women did not have the same rights as white males because people believed that they were not humans. They got some semblance of equality (e.g., franchise) barely a century ago.

Abrahamic religions want a stark distinction between apes and humans because of their theological claim that humans have a soul but animals do not. Historically, they defined a human as someone who could write a lawbook to produce a covenant with God. Since apes cannot write a book, therefore, they cannot have a covenant with God. Hence, they must not have a soul and they cannot be equated to humans. Humans and apes had to belong to different species due to covenant theology. Now as science sees similarities between humans and apes all these assumptions are called into question creating a big science-religion problem. These problems are closely tied to the historical theological dogmas.

The Vedic Attitude Toward Evolution

These problems don't exist in the Vedic system because it acknowledges 400,000 species of humans. It could include apes. The stark distinction between humans and apes—as those with and without a soul—doesn't exist in the Vedic system because it accepts that the foundation of all life is a soul. We are not able to clearly determine whether apes and humans belong to the same family because the basis of classifying species in the Vedic system is the mind rather than the body. Meaning and intentionality come before the body. Reductionism, materialism, and axiomatic reasoning are false. Life is created due to the presence of a soul with meaning and purpose. However, we are presently unable to construct a complete tree of life based on different meanings and purposes. This is not a problem that requires us to say that humans and apes belong to different families. Our minds could be similar to apes relatively speaking—i.e., in contrast to six other families of trees, reptiles, fishes, birds, insects, and beasts.

Therefore, if someone says that humans and apes belong to the same family, the Vedic system has no problem. After all, there are 8,400,000 species which are divided into seven families, and apes and humans could be parts of the human family that comprises 400,000 species. All these species don't exist in the same time and place. They appear and disappear. The loss of previous species is not a problem.

The disagreement is very simple—the species do not evolve from other species through random mutation and natural selection. They appear in large numbers quickly, akin to Cambrian Explosions. They co-evolve with other species because all species exist in ecosystems rather than in isolation. They have intended states because the meaning and purpose predates the appearance of the body. They are destroyed if they deviate from the intended state due to activation of dormant self-destructive elements. The appearance and disappearance of species involves meaning, intentionality, and ecosystems.

The Vedic Position on Evolution

Thus, the Vedic system doesn't oppose evolution. It opposes

the theory of evolution, which means the axioms of reductionism, materialism, axiomatic reasoning, random mutation, and natural selection. This is followed by a theory of evolution based on meaning, intentionality, collective adaptation, and self-destruction. Hence, bundling the Abrahamic religious opposition to evolution with the Vedic opposition to evolutionary theory is equating chalk with cheese because both of these appear to be white.

The Vedic system doesn't just oppose evolutionary theory. It also opposes the germ theory of medicine. The main cause of disease is not germs infecting an organism in the Vedic system. The core cause is the deviation of an organism from its intended state which activates self-destructive elements within the organism. Thereby, diseases are spontaneously generated in a body that has deviated from the intended state. Accordingly, the system of medicine conformant to this theory of spontaneous generation tries to restore the body to its intended state. That restoration automatically kills any potential germs.

Similarly, new species are spontaneously generated within an ecosystem. They are like useful or harmful bacteria or viruses in our body. They exist in a dormant potential form and are activated either because the ecosystem needs them to serve useful purposes or because the ecosystem has deviated from its intended state and previously dormant harmful elements in the ecosystem have to be activated to have the ecosystem self-destruct. The spontaneous generation of species requires us to treat an ecosystem just like a living body, and species in that ecosystem like useful and harmful ingredients within it.

Thus, the principles of biology and ecology are not different. The principles of spontaneous generation from a dormant state are not different from the activation of dormant potentials in physics. The theories of biological evolution are consistent with the theories of social and civilizational evolution. Each subject informs the other subjects and allows us to reconcile it into a single coherent theory of reality.

The basic difference is very simple—organisms are self-correcting, self-defending, and self-creating. No axiomatic reasoning system is self-correcting, self-defending, and self-creating. No self-correcting, self-defending, and self-creating machine can be created. No mathematical theory can replicate the simplest and most obvious properties of an organism. No materialistic, reductionistic, or mechanistic theory can explain organisms because all such theories are rooted in axiomatic reasoning systems. The dogmatic scientific institutions are unable to accept that their entire edifice stands on a bad foundation.

Indifference to Materialistic Ideas

The institutionalization of materialism, reductionism, axiomatic reasoning, random mutation, and natural selection in modern academics doesn't bother the followers of the Vedic system because ER-like seeds of self-destruction are inbuilt into every organism, institution, society, ecosystem, and civilization. They lie dormant until they are spontaneously reactivated when a system deviates from its intended state.

When organisms, institutions, societies, ecosystems, and civilizations perish due to deviation from the intended states, they have nobody but themselves to blame. Of course, their leaders make valiant attempts to shift the blame to external factors. They equate their bad personal choices to random mutations and the self-destruction that follows to natural selection by environmental factors. They claim to have been killed by external germs rather than their personal self-destructive choices. Such theories or explanation are nothing more than deceitful attempts to escape responsibility for one's choices.

We have to replace random mutation with choice and natural selection with responsibility for a choice. Individual and collective evolution occurs as the result of choice and responsibility. There is a science of choice and responsibility. It is not based on materialism, reductionism, axiomatic reasoning, random mutation, and natural selection. It is rather based on meaning, intention, choices, and their judgment.

Nature is not devoid of meaning, purpose, choice, or judgment. Such claims are institutionalized lies created by people who did not want to be held responsible for their choices. The Vedic system doesn't respect those who try to escape responsibility. It doesn't equate the exceptional power of institutions to truth. It disregards the power of institutionalized falsehoods because it knows that the seeds of self-destruction lie within. External forces are unnecessary to stop a system that will self-destruct as the result of its bad choices. The Vedic system truthfully informs people about the impending doom and leaves them free to choose their destiny, because its model of reality is choice and responsibility.

Does Decoherence Solve the Quantum Problem?

Quantum mechanics creates a problem of Realism because of the assumption (since Greek times) that each thing is just one thing. This axiom breaks in quantum mechanics because each thing is a collection of multiple possibilities. This problem has resisted a solution because it is widely and incorrectly supposed that macroscopic objects are just one thing and the problem of multiple possibilities is unique to subatomic particles. Attempts to solve this problem therefore focus on how multiple possibilities become just one. Decoherence is one such attempt. In this post, I will discuss why the classical physical assumption about reality (that it is just one thing) is false even for macroscopic objects before talking about how Decoherence tries to address this issue although it is not a genuine solution to the problem.

Let's begin with a macroscopic object to illustrate the problem of multiple possibilities. Suppose that you have a pen in your hand. Most people, most of the time, would call it a pen. In such cases, we can say that the thing in question is just one thing, and the classical realist assumption that one thing is just one thing is true. However, occasionally, we can also use that pen as a toy, paperweight, doorstop, weapon, and so on. Suppose we take into account all these uses. In that case, the classical assumption of Realism fails because whatever we called a pen earlier is in fact a collection of possibilities, with the pen only being more likely than a toy, paperweight, doorstop, weapon, and so on. In fact, whether something is treated as one out of the many possibilities depends on the environment, the user, the specific situation, etc.

Now, we have to say that the thing in question is *ideally* a pen, but *possibly* other things. Ideality is not subjective; we can also define it objectively. For instance, the pen will not work as an ideal toy, paperweight, doorstop, or weapon. A gun is a much better weapon; a large and heavy object is a much better paperweight; something that offers much more resistance is a much better doorstop; and a radio-controlled car is a much better toy. The pen, on the other hand, works ideally only as a pen. By putting each thing to the test of what it works as ideally, we can conclude what each thing is. Since this test can be performed by anyone, therefore, ideality is objective. And yet, we cannot determine the ideality without comparing what something does to what other things do. Something is ideally a pen only in contrast to infinite other things. Therefore, even as ideality is an innate property of the thing in question, it cannot be *known* by observing the pen in isolation.

This requires us to revise Realism in several ways: (a) reality is ideality, (b) ideality is innate, and (c) ideality is known through contrasts. If we don't know what something is ideally, we can use it in many possible ways. Since this applies to every macroscopic object, therefore, the quantum measurement problem doesn't disappear for macroscopic objects, unless we *choose* to *use* each thing in only one way. Realism holds true in the macroscopic case only because we typically choose to use everything in one way. Since that is a choice that "collapses" many possibilities into one, therefore, the macroscopic reality is also the result of an observer making a choice to collapse possibilities.

This basic property of collapse through an interaction is used in Decoherence. The environment or observer is treated as yet another quantum system with its own possibilities. When two sets of possibilities interact, the possibility common between them becomes *more likely*, while possibilities not common between them become *less likely.* The system now reduces to the more likely possibility, which appears to be a collapse. The important thing is that this kind of collapse doesn't require a non-material consciousness. It just requires another quantum system. This is why many proponents of Decoherence say that they have "solved" the quantum measurement problem.

But before we accept Decoherence as a solution to the quantum problem, let's try to understand the principle involved through an intuitive example of two humans interacting with each other.

Suppose a husband is the possibility of watching a movie or going shopping, while a wife is the possibility of reading a book or going shopping. When the husband-wife possibilities intersect, both of them go shopping because it is the common possibility between them. Through their interaction, possibilities are reduced to actuality. In this reduction, we don't have to suppose that the husband or the wife is a "consciousness". We can also say that they are two quantum ensembles that interact with each other, which causes their possibilities to intersect, which reduces them to a common possibility, which becomes the observed actuality.

We can extend this example by varying the *likelihood* of possibilities. We can say that the husband's likelihood of going shopping is 0.1 while his likelihood of watching a movie is 0.9. Similarly, we can say that the wife's likelihood of going shopping is 0.5 and the likelihood of reading a book is 0.5. Due to husband-wife interaction, both go shopping even though the husband on his own would have most likely watched a movie. Thereby, even an unlikely event becomes actuality by a combination of two sets of possibilities. However, if the husband were to spend his time with a male friend with a similar likelihood of possibilities, then both would likely watch a movie, instead of going shopping.

Once we understand the principle behind Decoherence, then we have to recognize that choices are still involved. For example, there is a choice for a husband to be with a wife or a male friend. Once the choice of companion has been made, then the subsequent outcomes are determined by the commonalities between the interacting companions. Thus, Decoherence doesn't eliminate choice. It only shifts the choice from the activity one wants to do to the companion one wants to be with. Instead of saying that a husband decides what to do, we say that he chooses to be with someone. Their interaction then naturally produces an actuality. The choice is now the selection of a companion.

Decoherence is a general pattern under which *circumstances* force choices on us. Given a circumstance, our options are so limited that we are compelled to act in a specific manner. We say that we had no choice in the matter. It is true. To make different choices, we have to change our circumstances. For example, if we don't want the alternatives forced on us by a bad company, then we have to change our company. In a different company, we will automatically make different choices. But that is not the elimination of choice. It is just a different kind of choice. The circumstances that force choices on us are not "given". The process of changing the circumstances to change the choice can be long and complex, and certainly harder than making a choice within the circumstances, but a choice made with hardship is still a choice.

Whenever there is a choice, there is indeterminism. Decoherence doesn't solve the indeterminism, although it shifts the indeterminism from a state within a quantum system to the choice of another quantum system. Since the universe is infinite such systems, each quantum system can decohere with infinite other quantum systems, to produce infinite different actualities. For there to be one out of infinite actualities, each system must select the quantum systems it decoheres with. The sequence of mutual interactions cannot be predicted by a mathematical formula. Therefore, Decoherence isn't a solution to the quantum problem; it is merely the replacement of one problem with another.

The Failure of Mechanization

The Failed Mechanization of Everything

The Meaning and Uses of Algorithms

An algorithm is a sequence of steps that begins with receiving an input and ends with generating an output. We can merge many such sequences into one, interspersed with decisions, depending on the input. For instance, we can follow one sequence of steps for inputs less than some chosen number and another sequence of steps for inputs greater than that chosen number. An algorithm appears complex if it is interspersed with many decisions. However, under the hood, it is always a linear sequence of steps based on the input. The combination of an algorithm and an input is therefore always deterministic.

Since an algorithm is a linear sequence of steps, it can be programmed into a machine in a linear sequence of steps. This machine is called a computer and the algorithm given to a machine is called a program. The computer has a bootloader program to receive other programs. It receives these programs and stores them just like data. It executes these programs just like algorithms. All that can be done with mathematics can be done with algorithms, and vice versa. All that can be done with algorithms can be done with machines, and vice versa. Conversely, all that cannot be done with mathematics also cannot be done with algorithms, and vice versa. All that cannot be done with algorithms also cannot be done with machines, and vice versa. Mathematics, algorithms, and machines are functionally equivalent.

The Failed Mechanization of Knowledge

Modern science began with the attempt to mechanize knowledge. The Scientific Method was defined as a wheel with a handle. This wheel comprised three main steps: (a) make observations, (b) formulate theory, and (c) make predictions. The handle on the wheel was meant to iterate through these steps. The input to this machine was observations, and the output was predictions. In between these two were theories based on generalizing the observations and using them to make predictions.

It was believed that through the successive iterations of the wheel of observations, theories, and predictions, the number of predictions will increase while the number of theories will decrease and, eventually, we will be able to explain all observations with one universal theory of reality. As we got closer to the universal theory, we would make fewer changes to the theory, while the predictions made by the theory would cover larger domains of observable phenomena. This belief was never proven.

Experience has instead shown that as we turn the wheel of the Scientific Method, we oscillate between opposites. Some phenomena require one type of theory while other phenomena require the opposite type of theory. If we try to merge these opposites into a single theory, we get probabilistic predictions. Over time, the number of opposite theories increases. When these opposites are merged into a single theory, we get multidimensional probabilistic theories. The theory gets less and less useful over time because the predictions become less and less certain. Expanding the theory is counterproductive.

Since physics has been the overarching paradigm for every area of modern science, therefore, we can illustrate this problem with physics. Physics began with Newton's mechanics. The universe was modeled as particles. Then many kinds of wave phenomena were discovered, light being the most prominent. The universe had to be sometimes modeled as particles and sometimes as waves. The merger of these two opposite models of reality resulted in a probabilistic theory called quantum mechanics. Meanwhile, it was discovered that the theory of space-time contradicts the theory called quantum mechanics. The former is continuous matter while the latter is discrete matter. The former is a local theory and the latter is a non-local theory. No attempt to resolve this contradiction has been successful thus far.

An attempt called String Theory was made to merge all matter and force into a multidimensional theory. However, it required many new parameters due to which it was no longer just one theory. String Theory became a euphemism for 10^{500} theories. The universe is at most 10^{80} particles. It has at most existed for 10^{18} seconds. It is at most 10^{23} meters across. The space, time, and matter in the universe are not enough to pick one out of 10^{500} theories. The wheel of the Scientific Method can no longer be turned because the universe is too small to select one out of the huge number of possible theories.

The Failed Mechanization of the Workforce

Industrialization extended mechanical modeling to humans. Each human, it was assumed, is like a blank computer at birth. It has a bootloader, which we call its learning ability. If this human is sent to a classroom, his bootloader can be used to gradually load it with new programs. Since the programs are sequential, therefore, they can be loaded sequentially. Since the complex algorithms use simple algorithms, therefore, simple programs had to be loaded before complex programs. The loading of simple programs was primary education and the loading of complex programs was advanced education.

A more educated human was one loaded with more complex programs. As the human finished the process of loading a certain type of program, he became a machine suitable for a certain type of job role in the industrial system of economics. Each person entering the industrial workforce was paid according to the type of programs that had previously been loaded into them during education.

It was assumed that this process of education would suffice. However, experience showed that any general model has infinite exceptions. Students coming out of the classroom were trained in general models, that had infinite exceptions. Their education fell infinitely short of reality. As they tried to match up to reality through on-job training, they realized the need for integrating logically opposite models, with each opposite model being used selectively for different inputs. As more and more models are integrated based on different inputs, the total complexity grows exponentially along with the cost.

The benefit of this extraordinary complexity is not proportional to the cost. Every new problem takes more time, effort, and money, but its benefits are not proportional. This puts the workforce under great pressure. It seems that the workforce is ineffective because when complexity grows, it takes more time, effort, and money to produce anything. Eventually, the workforce is replaced by machines. Now, a new problem arises: The producers are also consumers; if producers are replaced by machines, then there is nobody to consume the products created by machines, and the entire economic system collapses.

The Failed Mechanization of Products

Since a general model has infinite exceptions, and since those exceptions cannot be handled upfront, therefore, flawed products are put out and then improved over time. This means, what economists call, *creative destruction*. The old has to be replaced with the new to make things better. This generates a lot of unrecyclable garbage. Thus, as we undergo the process of creative destruction, eventually the earth becomes a landfill of garbage ending the possibility of creating anything new. In fact, as land, water, and air are endlessly polluted by unrecyclable garbage, we must eventually run out of food for humans.

Natural processes are cyclical because what is food for one organism is waste for another and what is waste for one organism is food for another. The food for an organism is always an organism. The waste created by an organism is always organisms that can become food for other organisms. Organisms are non-mechanistic entities. They have the capacity for self-correction, self-defense, self-control, and self-education. A large organism comprises smaller organisms, with the above organismic capacities.

When machines input organisms, they destroy their organismic properties and produce inorganic waste. This is because mathematics lacks the organismic properties of self-defense, self-correction, self-control, and self-education. The products of a machine are dead bodies and not living organisms. As we consume these dead bodies, our organismic capacity (self-correction, self-learning, self-control, and self-defense) rapidly declines. By eating dead bodies, our body becomes weak and susceptible to disease.

The output of a machine cannot become food for another organism. What cannot be food for another organism is waste. If this waste is consumed, the organism is weakened. If the waste is not consumed, the waste accumulates and reduces the capacity for food. Over time, industrial processes convert a living ecosystem into dead garbage. That is because organisms consume waste, are weakened by that waste, and die because they cannot defend against that waste. Industrialization slowly kills life.

Causes of the Failing Mechanization

The Law of Diminishing Returns

Through the above examples, we can see the problems of mathematics, algorithms, and machines. The knowledge system based on mathematics dies because the time, space, and matter required to produce a useful theory exceeds the age, size, and matter of the universe. The economy based on mathematics dies because the cost and complexity increase continuously, the benefits don't increase proportionately, and attempts to match cost to benefits remove the consumers from the economy. The ecosystem of life consumed and produced by machines dies because too much unrecyclable waste is produced which destroys both the capacity to produce nutritious food and the consumers of that nutritious food.

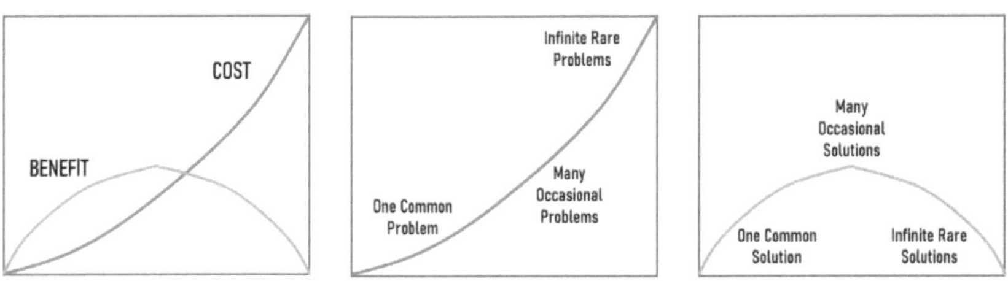

The entire situation can be summarized through the Law of Diminishing Returns. When we create a general mathematical model of reality, there are infinite exceptions to the model. The exceptions result in failures. To address those failures, we must continuously change the general model increasing its complexity and cost. However, most unique situations occur rarely. The benefits of adding those unique situations to the general model yield a rare benefit. The cost of each unique situation is high. However, the benefit of solving these unique situations is low. Hence, when we try to solve problems, over time, the costs keep growing while benefits keep declining. This is called the Law of Diminishing Returns.

The Reasons for Diminishing Returns

The benefits of costs are not always proportional. In the beginning, a small cost gives many benefits. Then, the cost and benefits are equal. Eventually, costs outrun benefits. This is because, in the beginning, we solve for a common case. It costs something but it has a huge benefit because the case is common. But as time passes by, we find exceptions to the common case, which occur occasionally. Solving these problems matches the costs with benefits. Then we start facing rare problems. The cost of solving these problems is still high. But because that situation occurs rarely, hence, the benefits are very low.

Factually, a common case is relative to a time, place, situation, and person. There is nothing common across the universe. The common case is just the local case. It seems common to the local people. Its cost is low and its benefits are local. If we stick to local production and consumption, then everyone gets enough of what they need locally. When the solution is localized, then the benefits exceed the costs. We cannot globalize this solution. The producers and consumers of the solution must be local.

Problems arise while trying to globalize a locally useful solution. We have to fix infinite problems in order to do that. The cost of doing that is infinite. But even if we did it, the benefits would still be finite. Hence, the globalization of a locally useful solution leads to diminishing returns. The correct approach is to use different local solutions for local problems. Of course, that limits the use of the solution. It means the localization of the economy. It also means the lowering of the costs. However, if a general model is used, the costs become infinite but the benefit remains finite because the general model doesn't fit infinite unique situations. Then, one unsolved problem becomes catastrophic in an unforeseen situation.

Failure Rooted in Mathematical Models

The overarching assumption in science and industrialization is that reality is mathematical. Whatever is mathematical is algorithmic and mechanical. Mathematical modeling assumes that reality is *uniform*. That things are the same for all times and places. This is a false assumption. No two apples are the same. No two people are the same. No two times are the same. No two places are the same. Reality is infinitely unique. When we try to fit this infinite uniqueness into a universal mathematical model, we get infinite exceptions to the rule. The cost of handling these exceptions grows rapidly over time. Old things have to be replaced by new things because the old things don't handle the exceptions as often expected.

As the cost and complexity of exceptions increase beyond the benefits, even more waste is generated. It could be wasteful theories. It could be wasteful people. It could be wasteful products. This waste cannot be recycled. We cannot use wasteful theories to make better theories. We cannot use wasteful people to produce better people. We cannot use wasteful products to produce better products. As time passes, the waste increases. That in turn destroys people, theories, and products, ending the ecosystem.

The assumption of uniformity, mathematics, algorithms, and machines proves extremely deceptive. It looks good in the beginning and it proves fatal in the end. This problem results from the attempt to create a general model of reality, under the assumption that reality is uniform everywhere, although reality is infinitely unique. The assumption that reality is uniform is called *universalism*. Under universalist thinking, people try to create mathematical models of reality. In the social sphere, they try to create laws for a society or nation. It works well in the beginning. As time passes, exceptions to these models and laws are discovered. Then the models and laws are updated. Then, the exceptions to the established models and laws require logically opposite models and laws. To combine these logical opposites into a single mathematical theory, we need per-input decisions. If we cannot make such decisions, then the result is a probabilistic, indeterministic, and statistical model. Now we cannot predict and explain.

The Alternative to Mathematical Models

The alternative to mechanism is an organism. The alternative to uniformity is uniqueness. The alternative to inorganic is organic. Everything begins by saying that reality is not objects but persons. Each person is unique. Persons have the capacity for self-control, self-learning, self-improvement, and self-defense, so they are not machines. Each person has unique knowledge, talents, and motivations. Hence, they cannot be reduced to a common mathematical model. A person inputs and outputs organically. The waste for one person is food for another person, which recycles waste. If we produce and consume that which can be fully recycled, we never run out of resources. The society, ecosystem, and planet become stable.

In this zone of stability, security, and safety, living entities become free of fear. Now, they pursue the truth because they are not afraid for their survival. That truth is based on the understanding that all reality is personal, and each person is many tiers of reality. The persons are also organized in many tiers. To know the truth, we have to traverse the tiers within a person and between the persons. The process of truth involves going from a lower truth to a higher truth. The lower truth is the surface truth; the higher truth is the deeper truth. Even as we can observe the surface truths, we cannot understand why they are necessary. The necessity of a surface truth is established by the deeper truth. As we progress in this hierarchy of truths, we arrive at the Supreme Truth.

Mechanistic thinking believes in a Universal Truth—one formula for all times, places, situations, and persons. Organismic thinking believes in a Supreme Truth—one source of infinite diversity that creates unity in diversity. In short, we replace *uniformity* with *unity in diversity*.

An Alternative Criterion for Supreme Truth

Many people ask: How can we be sure that the hierarchy of truth isn't an infinite cascade of truths? What terminates this hierarchy into a Supreme Truth? The answer to this question is personalism. A higher truth must not just provide a justification for a lower truth but it must also be a greater happiness. That is because the truth is a person. The highest truth is the greatest happiness. Ideas are not self-justified. But happiness is self-justified. We don't need to give an explanation, justification, or necessity for happiness. It is self-evident. Hence, if we talk only about truths, the highest level of truth is not self-justified. However, if that truth is also happiness, then the truth is self-justified.

In short, the Supreme Truth must be the Supreme Person, if there has to be any truth. His happiness is the justification, necessity, and explanation for everything else that is a lower truth. This is the personalization of truth. We might ask: How do we know that some person is the Supreme Person? The answer is the limit to our happiness. By knowing a lower truth, we get some happiness. But knowing a higher truth, we get more happiness. The limit to that happiness is knowing the Supreme Truth. Everyone can know whether some truth is the Supreme Truth by measuring their own happiness. This is a first-person, unmediated, direct, and unfalsifiable condition for knowing.

The study that begins in treating reality as persons, ends in the Supreme Person, as we search for the explanation, necessity, and justification for lower-level persons into higher-level persons. Conversely, the study that begins by treating reality as machines, mathematics, and algorithms end up with nothing. The failure of universalism leads to nihilism. The success of personalism leads to the Supreme Person. The failure of universalism converts life into death. The success of personalism converts an unhappy life into a happy life. Those who understand this difference need not worry about the problems created by universalism. Instead, they should focus on understanding personalism.

Comparative Evolutionary Timelines

While there are huge differences between the Vedic system and modern science on the origin of planets and how life appears in them, the differences are smaller when it comes to the age estimates for Earth, the age of the species, and the categorization of species into six major classes. For the latter, the biggest differences between the two descriptions are in species timelines. Specifically, in the Vedic system, the six major classes of species appear in quick succession while in modern science they are separated by millions of years. In this short article, I will discuss the consequences of this species separation.

Modern evolutionary theory is not cast in stone; as new evidence emerges the theory is modified. However, there is strong resistance to altering the timeline and sequence of species despite contrary evidence because change is disruptive to the evolutionary narrative. If the narrative quickly adapted to the new evidence, it would be highly unstable. Hence, there is much-overlooked counterevidence to create the impression that the evolutionary narrative is stable. Of particular interest in this article is the issue of millions of years of gaps between the advent of the six major classes of species that form the backbone of the evolutionary theory. These gaps lead to the question of how one class of species existed without the others when the evidence at present suggests a high interdependence between these classes.

The Vedic Description of Species

In the Vedic tradition, the body of a species is an effect of the mind. Each person creates their mind through their choices over lifetimes. Based on their mind, they get a body. The term jāti, or class, used for species, therefore, pertains primarily to the mind and secondarily to the body. Hence, a person in a human body can sometimes be called an animal, if their mind resembles animals more than humans. While the mind may not be perceived by others, its effects—i.e., the body—are perceivable. Thereby, the body is simply a way to know the mind, the deeper cause that explains and predicts the effects.

The relation between mind and body in the Vedic tradition is similar to that between a body and a shirt. Ideally, a shirt must fit the body perfectly. But if the shirts are standardized, then each person has to wear a best-match rather than a perfect-match shirt. In the same way, in regards to species, the body assigned to a mind may not be a perfect match for the mind. The body may have abilities that the mind may not want to utilize or the mind may have desires that the body may not be able to fulfill.

The Vedic tradition describes 8,400,000 standard bodies, divided into six classes. They are the best-fit rather than perfect-fit coverings of the mind. Nature resolves the misfit between the mind and the body (analogous to that between a body and a shirt) in successive births by assigning each type of mind a better-fitting body (analogous to a person discarding a misfit shirt and accepting a better-fitting shirt).

Brahma, the creator of living forms in the universe, *designed* 8,400,000 types of bodies. But all these bodies are not visible at all times, quite like all types of shirts are not always present in a clothing store, even if they have been designed. The visibility of a body depends on the current demand for that body, i.e., if there is a suitable mind to fit into a body. As various kinds of bodies appear and disappear, we don't call that the evolution of the bodies; it is rather a function of changing demands and supplies for bodies, quite like the changing shirts in a clothing store are not the result of one type of shirt evolving into another but rather a result of the changing demand and supply for various types of shirts.

The Vedic Description of Evolution

The trends of types of minds and bodies change over time. Time is therefore described both in terms of changing minds and bodies. There is a 4,320,000-year cycle called Chaturyuga, embedded in a cycle of 71 Chaturyuga called a Manvantara, embedded in a cycle of 14 Manvantara called a Kalpa. These three cycles are most relevant to the question of evolution because (a) at the end of one Manvantara, lasting about 306 million years, most life is destroyed and recreated, and (b) at the end of each Kalpa, lasting about 4.32 billion years, all life is destroyed and recreated thereafter. The present age is described as one after the elapse of 27 Chaturyuga and 9 Kali-Yuga in a Manvantara, and 6 Manvantara in a Kalpa. That means we should talk about a smaller and a bigger explosion of species with the following timeline:

- Smaller Explosion: 27 * 4,320,000 + 9 * 432,000 years = 121 million years
- Bigger Explosion: 6 * 306 million + 121 million = 2 billion years

The bigger explosion of species pertains to the advent of the Earth, at the beginning of a Kalpa. The smaller explosion of species pertains to the advent of most life forms at the beginning of a Manvantara. Geological and biological timelines are thus interrelated because even a planet is considered a living form. In ancient cultures, the Earth was called a mother who gave birth to various species. She wasn't like other mothers who could give birth only to one type of species but she was a mother nevertheless. The advent of the Earth is the advent of a mother at the beginning of a Kalpa. After that, the advent of the species is the advent of various children of the mother, at the beginning of a Manvantara.

The Vedic Description of Timelines

One of the basic properties of cyclical time is that it doesn't go uniformly in terms of change, creating a difference between *clock time* and *change time* (the change is conscious experience, so we can also call it clock time and conscious time). Even as Kali-Yuga, the current age, is 1/4th of Satya-Yuga, change in Kali-Yuga occurs four times faster than in Satya-Yuga. If we make the current rates of change the standard for measuring time, then the rate of change is 3/4th in Dvapara, 2/4th in Treta, and 1/4th in Satya. To extend the current rates of change for time in the distant past, we must apply the following corrections:

- Satya: 4x slower than Kali-Yuga for 4/10th of the Chatur-yuga duration
- Treta: 3x slower than Kali-Yuga for 3/10th of the Chatur-yuga duration
- Dvapara: 2x slower than Kali-Yuga for 2/10th of the Chaturyuga duration
- Kali: 1x slower than Kali-Yuga for 1/10th of the Chaturyuga duration

We can average out these differences over the long run to say that change occurs 4*4/10 + 3*3/10 + 2*2/10 + 1*1/10 = 3x slower than the current rate of change, which means to get accurate durations over the long run in terms of the current standards of time measurement, we must multiply the above periods by 3. Thus, the Earth is 6 billion years old based on the current rates of change although it is 2 billion years old based on Vedic time calculation. The life on Earth is about 363 million old based on current rates of change although it is 121 million years old based on the Vedic time calculation.

The Six-Tier Pyramid of Vedic Species

As noted above, the 8,400,000 species are divided into six major classes. They are described below.

- Those that live in water (called fishes, but include turtles, corals, and bacteria)
- Those that are non-moving (called plants and trees, but include creepers)
- Those that crawl on the ground (called reptiles, but include ants and spiders)

- Those that fly in the air (called birds, but include insects like flies and bees)
- Those that have four legs (called beasts, which include domestic and wild)
- Those that are born of humans (called humans, but are highly variegated)

Variety in the Vedic system is conceived in two ways: (a) pyramidal hierarchy, and (b) spokes of a wheel. This is a general pattern, not unique to species of life. For instance, a society is conceived as a pyramid and as a wheel. In a society of four classes, the upper class is more important than the lower. And yet, the upper class doesn't persecute the lower classes because they are the interdependent spokes of a wheel. The parts of a body are conceived as a pyramid and as a wheel. The head is more important than the stomach, hands, and legs, but the head doesn't persecute the other parts because it depends on them. The different aspects of a person's life are conceived as a pyramid and as a wheel. A spiritual purpose of life is most important, but it doesn't mean that the spiritual purpose persecutes the other activities of providing food, clothing, shelter, government, or entertainment because they are interdependent. Similarly, different species exist in a hierarchy and are interdependent spokes of a wheel.

Alternative Conceptions of Order

Other systems of philosophy influenced by the Vedic tradition accepted these two models of variety but tried to marginalize one of them. For instance, Buddhists accepted the idea of variety as a wheel but were not so enthusiastic about the concept of a pyramid. They tried to flatten the pyramid, equalizing all the spokes of a wheel and the result was that Buddhists gradually lost warriors, businessmen, and artisans because everyone aspired to become a monk. When these monks were attacked by invaders, they did not have warriors to protect them and so the result of flattening the pyramid was destruction.

Classical societies in the West were both pyramids and wheels. But as time passed, the higher classes began oppressing the lower classes. Society was no longer a wheel with many interdependent spokes as nobles and elites exploited and subjugated all other spokes. Then when these societies were attacked, the persecuted classes joined the attackers instead of defending the nobles and elites from them. After this, Western societies tried to eliminate the hierarchy, broke the spokes of the wheel into independent things, and called competition—rather than cooperation—the only good way of organizing life. The individualism of Western society is reflected in science as the independence of material things. Every man struggling for his own survival in Western society appears in evolutionary biology as each species struggling for its survival and evolving independently of other species to facilitate its survival.

The Western models of individualism and competition have worked for a short while on societies that were previously collectivist and cooperative, but gradually neglected their pyramid and wheel models of order and started thinking that these were unnecessary. As their inner pyramids and wheels became weak, they were divided and attacked by greedy societies that had used pyramids and wheels to become united. The attacker's success is not due to individualism and competition, as they like to tell everyone, but rather the result of their collectivism and cooperation, to conquer other weaker societies that had lost their inner unity precisely due to declining collectivism and cooperation. But this is not a permanent situation if the previously divided are again united and the previously united are again divided.

Since time immemorial, wise societies have talked about strength in unity. That requires pyramids and wheels. The Western conception of order as something produced out of individualism and competition is not true because it is always weaker than a united society. Evolutionary biology is not a true picture of order in nature. It is certainly not the way wise and traditional societies have conceived order. It is simply a Western construct, a byproduct of Western history, which was elevated to truth as long as Western societies could unite to attack divided societies. If the attacked societies unite and Western society divides, the process will reverse, and order will again be unity defined by pyramids and wheels.

Pyramid and Wheel of Six Classes

The six Vedic classes of species exist in pyramidical ecosystems, which gradually grow in width and height over time. This means that an ecosystem appears with a small number of species at the bottom of the pyramid and quickly a smaller second layer of species is added. With this addition, the bottom layer expands, and a third layer of species is added, which causes the second and the bottom layer to expand further, and then a fourth layer of species is added. This is an iterative process in which the pyramid cannot have a broad base without a tall vertex or a tall vertex without a broad base. The six classes mentioned above are layers on the pyramid so the highest species (i.e., humans) can appear after the lower species (fishes, plants, birds, reptiles, and beasts). However, since this process is iterative, humans are not the final stage of species appearance—i.e., the pinnacle of the evolutionary process. Instead, new types of fishes, plants, birds, reptiles, and beasts appear due to the appearance of humans.

Many people erroneously equate the Vedic description of the appearance of species to the Abrahamic creationist accounts although there are major differences. First, in the Abrahamic description, a species means a body while in the Vedic description, a species primarily means a mind and secondarily a body. Second, in the Abrahamic description, all species are created before the creation of humans while in the Vedic description, a small number of species in the lower five classes are created before humans (the sixth class) and the appearance of humans expands each of the lower five classes progressively. Third, humans have existed for a very long time because they quickly appeared after a small number of species in the lower five classes and saw the gradual appearance of many species in the lower five classes. Fourth, humans are not the pinnacle of the evolutionary process but an early milestone in it. Five, the Vedic description of the appearance of species is also evolutionary but iterative and not linear.

The correlation between the width and height of the pyramid makes the construction of any linear sequence of species extremely hard, and most such attempts will be flawed, leading to continuous adjustments to the linear sequence. For instance, some plants must appear before some insects. But if we don't have the fossil evidence for those plants that appeared earlier, we will connect the later appearing insects to those plants for which we have fossil evidence. It is a case of misattributing causality to the cause that we can find rather than the actual cause that we could not find. In this misattribution, we call Y the mother of Z because we haven't yet found the fossils for the actual mother X. But if X is found later, we will have to change the ancestry of both Y and Z, destabilizing the causal chain.

Modern evolutionary theories are linear which makes them highly unstable because as older fossils are discovered, the previous chain of causal events must be modified. Altering the causal chain is very hard if a later species depends on multiple previous species. The entire evolutionary description becomes worthless if the actual sequence is iterative while we are trying to construct a linear sequence.

Factually, no species exists by itself; it needs many other species to circulate nutrients. An ecosystem of species is a wheel with many spokes; the wheel's rotation is nutrient circulation. Thereby, an ecosystem of species is essential for any one species to exist. This, in turn, requires a sudden appearance of many species which contradicts the ideas of incremental change in modern evolutionary theories, even while this appearance is empirically observed (e.g., the Cambrian Explosion in modern biology). If change were indeed linear, all newly created species would die quickly because they depend on other species that don't exist currently. There would be no progress in evolution because of species interdependence.

The main problem of modern biology is that it is modeled after ideas of matter in classical physics: (a) inanimate objects can exist without other objects but in reality, living species do need other species, and (b) in physics an effect depends on a cause but the cause doesn't depend on the effect, whereas species actually have mutual interdependence. When the ideas of classical physics are extended to biology, chaos ensues. To construct any theory of biology, we have to discard the idea that life emerges from the lifeless. If life is fundamental, then pyramids and wheels are essential, change is collective and iterative rather than individual and linear, and all foundational ideas of modern biology are absurdly false.

The Six Classes of Modern Species

Modern evolutionary theory classifies the species in the same six categories as the Vedic tradition. However, these species begin millions of years apart, begging the question of how they survived without the other species. Just because we found fossil records of some species doesn't mean we have explained how they could exist without the other species. The absence of evidence is not the evidence of absence. The following are rough evolutionary timelines based on modern archeological fossil evidence:

- Fishes about 530 million years ago
- Plants about 460 million years ago
- Reptiles about 320 million years ago
- Mammals about 225 million years ago
- Birds about 150 million years ago
- Humans about 6 million years ago

This sequence has two major differences with the Vedic description: (a) the birds appear after mammals in the modern evolutionary theory and before the mammals in the Vedic tradition, and (b) these species are originating millions of years apart, implying that they could exist without the other species. Since the dates attributed to different species keep changing with the discovery of fossils, the first discrepancy is not serious; it is quite likely that a future fossil discovery will push the age of birds back to before the mammals. The bigger issue is the huge gaps between the timelines of the various classes of species.

For instance, can a large variety of fishes exist without plants? The fact is that plants produce oxygen within water, which the fish need to survive. Oxygen depletion is a common cause of fish death in ponds. Many fish eat plants or microbes that in turn grow on plants. If there are no plants, the fish won't have oxygen and food. Before we put a 70-million-year gap between fishes and plants, we ought to explain how fishes lived without plants. Similarly, insects and reptiles play key roles in pollination and seed dispersion, as the plant seeds eaten by insects and reptiles are dispersed through defecation. Many insects and reptiles carry pollens on their bodies to other plants. Before we put a 140-million-year gap between plants and insects/reptiles, we ought to explain how plants survived without reptiles and insects. Interdependence between species creates ecosystems of species with a wide variety of species. We don't get isolated species. We either get the entire ecosystem of species or no species at all.

The problem is that science doesn't look for such types of evidence because it is impossible to know what a species was eating based on its fossils or genetics. Even if we find that a species eats one thing at present, one could argue that perhaps it was eating something else at one time and then evolved into other things over time. Since we can neither confirm nor deny that, science relies on genetic and fossil evidence but cannot explain how one species existed without other species because not all the data—e.g., what a species was eating—is available and there is no easy way to get that data anyway.

Genetic and fossil evidence can only tell us that a species existed no later than the fossil or genetic date. It cannot tell us if they did not exist before that. However, if we think of life in terms of pyramids and wheels then we can see that even if we did not find genetic and fossil evidence for some species, that species must exist because other species whose evidence has been found depend on that species. The lower tier of a pyramid must appear before the higher tiers. Then higher and lower tiers must iterate to broaden the pyramid's base while increasing its height. This requires us to replace the ideas drawn from physics (i.e., a single particle can exist in isolation or that cause-effect is linear) with those drawn from biology (i.e., that species exist in ecosystems in which many species are mutually interdependent).

As long as biology tries to extend physics to species, it will be riddled with bad ideas that survive simply because the contradicting evidence hasn't been found. Nobody can be sure if or when that evidence will be found. Greater value is derived by proving why life is not reducible to lifelessness. The theoretical assumptions of biology have to be inverted before biological data can be interpreted correctly.

The basic necessity for biology can be described through an ordinary human example. We don't make 50 types of shirts, followed by 50 types of pants, followed by 50 types of shoes. Initially, we make one shirt, one pant, and one shoe. We need these three to survive, in order to produce more shirts, pants, and shoes. A man with only a shirt, and without a pant and shoe, will not live to make a pant, shoe, or another shirt. Then, we make shirts, pants, and shoes in proportion to each other. We also make shirts, pants, and shoes to mutually pair them. An additional shirt depends on the prior pant and shoe even though the new shirt doesn't look like a pant and shoe. The apparent similarity between shirts is not the only type of cause. The apparent dissimilarity between shirt, pant, and shoe is also a cause.

The Forgotten Seventh Class of Species

In the Vedic tradition, the pyramid of six classes of species rests on the seventh class of life called the Earth, which has the capacity to generate life from the elements called Earth, Water, Fire, Air, and Ether. The generation begins with the Ether in which a linguistic description of the body—which some people call *Intelligent Design*—is present. While the mind describes what the species *can be*, the body describes what it *cannot be*. The relation between the subjective and the objective is possibility and impossibility. Therefore, the linguistic description, or Intelligent Design, defines what the body cannot be.

A subset of the Ether becomes the Air, a subset of that becomes Fire, a subset of that becomes Water, and a subset of that becomes Earth. These five elements correspond to the sensations of sound, touch, sight, taste, and smell. Since mind and body are related as possibility and impossibility, there can be many expressions of a mind into many bodies because what something can be underdetermines what it cannot be. Since the five elements are progressively subsets, there can be many variations of the perceived body based on the same design because different subsets of negations can be used.

The Earth, or any other planet in the universe, is a part of the cosmic Ether, which means a subset of designs in the universe. The Earth is itself the Intelligent Designer because Earth means a subset of cosmic Ether, which means a subset of designs. All these designs exist as potentials in the Earthly Ether, which means they are not always observable. They are just like quantum potentials. Activating these potentials needs a choice and as we have seen, a bare minimum subset of potentials must be collectively activated for these to form a living ecosystem. Modern evolutionary theory relies on random mutations because (a) it has no notion of preexisting design potentials, and (b) it has no way to explain how some potentials are activated because matter in evolutionary theory is unconscious. Randomness is supposed to solve both problems like a monkey hitting the keys of a typewriter to produce the Complete Works of Shakespeare. Except in dogmatic circles, it is widely accepted that this process will take too long and produce infinitely more short-lived life forms than long-lived ones, contrary to the evidence. Intelligent Design is cited as a solution to this problem, but how that design is activated is unknown. That is because the Intelligent Designer is Earth herself, but those talking about Intelligent Design, from an Abrahamic perspective (and subtly hinting toward the monotheistic God as the designer), depersonalized the Earth many centuries ago. To bring Earth back as an Intelligent Designer, they have to reverse their claims.

Personalization of the Earth is, in the Vedic system, the substitute for the modern evolutionary concepts of random mutation and natural selection. The advent of species does not need random mutations because a preexisting design in the Ether is activated by the Earth. The advent of species does not need natural selection because a set of mutually compatible species are collectively activated by the Earth as a wheel. The layering of species in a pyramid and wheel does not need random mutation or natural selection because these layers are activated iteratively by the Earth. The intelligence in the Earth is the precise iterative sequence required to construct the pyramid-wheel. Once this is created, it becomes self-sustaining as the parts of the pyramid-wheel are interdependently sustaining each other. The pinnacle of the pyramid, i.e., the humans, should understand and preserve this pyramid-wheel for their own survival. The pinnacle is not expected to exploit, subjugate, or persecute the other parts of the pyramid-wheel because that is a sure way to destroy humanity and is the pinnacle of stupidity.

Vedic Theories vs. Christian Creationism

The step-by-step ideas of gradual evolution (the theory of genetic inheritance with slow modification) are already disproven based on the evidence of the Cambrian Explosions. Evolutionary theory today rests on the claims about the massive gaps between various classes of species but that claim—without explaining how these species existed without others—is premature. If instead, we relied on the model of pyramids and wheels, then the timeline gaps between species would be far narrower. While that may not be called a Cambrian Explosion, it would be the case of fast horizontal and vertical growth of the pyramid.

These ideas cannot be dismissed like Christian Creationism because the Earth in Christianity is only 6000 years old, and God created all species at once, which means 6000 years ago, when according to the Vedic system, the Earth is 6 billion years old and the current iteration of life originated 363 million years ago. Even as these timelines aren't equal to the timelines obtained by modern dating methods (which state that the Earth is 4.5 billion years old and life originated in a Cambrian Explosion around 530 million years ago), the two differ by 30% rather than by a factor of 80,000 (in case of the Christian creation of species) and 750,000 (in the case of the Christian creation of the universe). There has to be some idea of the magnitude of difference before we equate two things whimsically.

The Problem of Dogmatic Sciences

The Vedic system doesn't need any Western construct because it already has far better constructs with regard to mind and body, how the body is created based on the mind, the nature of space divided into various planets (called Graha or houses for residence), how each planet contains certain fixed types of designs about which species can be activated in that planet, how these designs are activated iteratively to create pyramid-wheels that become self-sustaining ecosystems, which intelligent humans sustain.

The problem arises only if unproven dogmas are forced on people without reason and evidence. That forced indoctrination has to be countered forcefully. The correct method of science is that we collect data and then try to explain it. The hypothesis comes after the data. But everyone has the data about their capacity to perceive, conceive, and judge right from birth. They don't need science to know that. However, science claims that we are nothing more than molecules without explaining how molecules create our perception, conception, and judgment. In so far as molecules are mathematics, and the mind is known to not be reducible to mathematics, scientific claims are not just the unproven, not just the unprovable, but the already disproven. Persisting with the disproven is a symptom of malintent.

The likely scenario is that there is something sinister in evolutionary biology in terms of obscuring, marginalizing, or discarding evidence that doesn't fit the evolutionary narrative, to preserve the appearance of truth, to perpetuate an immoral and materialistic ideology of life. This is nothing more than an adverse immune reaction to a long history of forced indoctrination into false religious dogmas. Just because some religions have forcibly indoctrinated people into unprovable claims and provably false lies, doesn't confirm the absence of perception, conception, and judgment. Just because some people endured false religious claims for centuries doesn't mean everyone's claims are false. The discovery of a liar doesn't make everyone a liar. But it does make a person who has been lied to distrust others.

We can sympathize with those who have been lied to and developed distrust for anything that sounds remotely similar. But that won't invalidate the fact that the replacement ideology being trusted currently is already disproven on both theoretical (the inability to reduce minds to mathematics or molecules) and empirical (the Cambrian Explosions of multiple species at once) grounds. The only leg on which evolution stands today is large gaps between species, which is also hugely problematic because these species cannot exist in isolation. Therefore, the solution cannot be either one of evolutionary theory vs. Christian Creationism because both are false. The real solution to the problem of being lied to and developing distrust is looking at alternatives not suffering from that problem. The Vedic tradition offers that opportunity for those interested.

www.ingramcontent.com/pod-product-compliance
Ingram Content Group UK Ltd.
Pitfield, Milton Keynes, MK11 3LW, UK
UKHW041313190726
13845UKWH00025B/232

9 789385 384523